HEAVEN
ON MY
MIND

bible
fact
points

BEST SELLING AUTHOR
BRYAN CUTSHALL

HEAVEN
ON MY
MIND

Heaven on My Mind
Copyright 2016 Church Trainer, Inc.
All rights reserved.

ISBN: 978-0-9855372-1-0

No part of this publication may be reproduced, transmitted in any form, translated into any language or by any means, electronic or mechanical, without permission in writing from the author.

Printed in the United States of America

Church Trainer, Inc.
P.O. Box 21792
Chattanooga TN 37424
(888) 366-6498

www.churchtrainer.com

Table of Contents

Forward		7
Introduction		9
Chapter 1	An Open Window	11
Chapter 2	The Open Door	15
Chapter 3	Eternal Life is a Real Life	19
Chapter 4	The Garment of Praise	25
Chapter 5	Fourteen Things that God Records and Rewards	29
Chapter 6	When God Made Adam and Eve, They Lived Naked? Are You Worried?	33
Chapter 7	Heaven is a Real Place, Not Life on a Cloud	37
Chapter 8	The Five Crowns Worn in Heaven	41
Chapter 9	No Lost Tears	49
Chapter 10	Paradise	61
Chapter 11	Peeking through Windows	69
Chapter 12	The Kings of Heaven	75
Chapter 13	Body Language	81

Chapter 14	To Infinity and Beyond	87
Chapter 15	Many Rooms	91
Chapter 16	Well Done	97
Chapter 17	Children in Heaven	101
Chapter 18	Will We Go to Church in Heaven?	105
Chapter 19	Living Water	109
Chapter 20	A New Name	113
Chapter 21	The Cloud of Witnesses	119
Chapter 22	Another View of Eternity	123
	Notes	127

Forward

I CANNOT RECALL WHEN I have read a more encouraging book than *Heaven on My Mind*. Dr. Bryan Cutshall has given us an amazing revelation on Heaven unlike anything you have ever read. A book that doesn't tickle your ears, but rather, ratchets up your faith. It is full of hope and promises for what awaits the child of God on the other side of those Pearly Gates. Read about: Coals of Fire, Books in Heaven, Rainbows, Sea of Glass, Rivers of Crystal Clear Water, Animals in Heaven, a Room Full of Tears in a Bottle and so much more. A book you won't be able to put down. A classic that should be in every Christian's library.

Marcus D. Lamb
Founder/President: Daystar Television Network

Introduction

I HAVE BEEN TALKING about this book on Heaven for a couple of years now. It is now finished! This book is different from many of the other books I have written. While it filled with many of the great heaven passages in the Bible that give us windows and doors into heaven, it is also filled with my glorified imagination. I tried to place myself in the rooms of heaven, the streets of heaven and with the people of heaven. We will be true to the scriptures, but this book will also let your imagination soar.

I am fascinated when I hear stories of people who died for a few minutes and came back to us with a glimpse of heaven. Conversations they've had, extraordinary things they've seen and done. I have heard of rose bushes that glisten and when a bloom is picked, another immediately comes back in its place. Stories like these have piqued my curiosity about what life may be like when we get there.

Most of the sermons I heard about heaven growing up were about the Great White Throne judgment and the whole world hearing about your sins. That just didn't sound like a very good place to live. I also heard some people describe heaven as though we were going to live on a cloud and play harps. That sounded boring to me.

I knew Jesus was going to be there, but after a few chats, songs and casting my crowns at His feet, what next? I was told I would be able to talk to the people in the Bible, as well as see all of my loved ones and friends who had died. To me, it seemed like a big church service with a huge lobby for telling stories.

All of that sounded good, but the hang up for me was the word *eternity*. Even if I spent 10 years talking to the Bible characters, family and friends, what would I do with the rest of eternity? Are there books to read? Horses to ride? Jetskis, boating, fishing, tubing? Are there neighborhoods, libraries, restaurants, swimming pools, and all of the things we like to do on this earth? Or is it just going to be the eternal worship service with the big lobby for story-telling?

So my quest continued. What would it be like to live in heaven?

I have to confess that while this book is filled with Scriptures and the absolute truth of God's Word, I have also used my imagination to interpret possible meanings for some of these heavenly scenes. Get ready for a colorful journey into heaven where sights, sounds and scenes come to life in your soul and spirit. By the time you finish this book, I hope you can say, "When we all get to heaven, what a day of rejoicing that will be!"[1]

CHAPTER 1

An Open Window

While there are literally hundreds of verses that refer to heaven or the heavens as a location, I was surprised to learn that the Old Testament Scriptures say almost nothing descriptive about heaven. The prophets Isaiah and Ezekiel both saw God on His throne, and there's the mention of a couple archangels and some seraphim. Isaiah 14 tells the story of Lucifer's fall and how he desired to sit in the mount of the congregation in the sides of the north, and Daniel saw two archangels and a battle in heaven... that's it. Yet, those amazing patriarchs died in their faith. They were tortured, thrown to the lions, killed by the sword, and lived nomadic lives all in the name of serving God, but never knew about heaven. It would seem their sacrifices were to please God and help bring about the kingdom of the Messiah, without knowledge of the afterlife. Think about *that!*

Fast forward into the New Testament: John 14:2-3. One day, Jesus was having a conversation with His disciples and declares something they've not heard before. ***In My Father's house are many mansions; if it were not so, I would have told you. I go to prepare a place for you. And if I go and prepare a place for you, I will come again and receive you to Myself; that where I am, there you may be also***. This teaching disrupted their thinking. Can you imagine the conversations that followed?

"Why'd He say that?"

"Didn't He say He had nowhere to lay His head—should we believe Him?"

It seemed far-fetched and was hard to understand. No one had ever taught this before. No Rabbi had taught of any such place.

The disciples continued to question Him about it, and on another occasion, they asked, "When is Your kingdom coming?" Jesus told them what to watch for, and in Luke 9:27, He said, **"But I tell you, there are some standing here who shall not taste death till they see the kingdom of God.**

In John 21, the third time following His resurrection that Jesus showed Himself to His disciples, Jesus was grilling more than fish on the beach that morning. Peter was in the hot seat as Christ questioned him about the depth and level of his love, then Jesus said, "...**when you are old, you will stretch out your hands, and another will gird you and carry you where you do not wish."** Peter understood this meant he would die a death of crucifixion. Then, as we are inclined to do when confronted with a perceived injustice, Peter looked at John, the youngest disciple, and asked, "What about him?" Jesus replied, **"If I will that he remain till I come, what is that to you?"** John 21 records this story and tells us that a saying went out from among the disciples that John could not die until he saw the kingdom of God come. Talk about pressure in the ministry, wow! How would you like to know that you can't die until...? Of course, we know that Jesus did *not* say John wouldn't die (verse 23).

Years passed and by 70 A.D., all of the disciples were dead, except guess who. That's right. John. He was still alive and the only apostle left leading the scattered and persecuted church. Also in that year, the Romans burned Jerusalem and the Jewish people began to scatter all over the world to escape persecution. But house churches kept popping up, and the Romans became furious that they could not stamp out the new religious sect of Christians. So they decided to stage the public execution of John in order to stop Christianity.

In 94 A.D., they filled a pot with boiling oil in the public square and pulled John high in the air on a rope and pulley. The Christians and Romans gathered to witness the event as they lowered the last remaining apostle, now an old man, into the pot. Then a miracle happened. The boiling oil had no effect on his body and the spillover that should have caused a blaze actually extinguished the fires. However, that miracle lit a new fire in the Christians. They left with new hope. The Roman government decided that John should be exiled to get him out of the eyes of the public. He was sent to a labor camp—a rock quarry—on the Turkish island of Patmos.

Every day, the old man would pick up large rocks and carry them to the pile. Using hammers, he'd break them up into stones to be used on Roman roads. The sun was hot, the days were long and the whip of a Roman overseer was striping his back as he carried large, back-breaking stones for hours and days and months that turned into years.

Forsaken! I am sure John felt what many others felt who have served God. What would your thoughts and questions be? *Does God know about this? Does He know where I am? After all, I helped feed the 5,000. I was there for all the miracles. I served the Master well. I went to the cross with Him and He even gave me the responsibility of caring for His mother. I did that and much more. I was there on the mountain with Peter and James when He transformed into His glorious body. I saw Him ascend into heaven. I have worked alone for years and I'm the only remaining apostle… and now this? Really? This is how the story ends? In a back-breaking, torturous, lonely labor camp?*

But because of what John had seen, he couldn't deny his faith. He was in pain every day, but still believed. He was praying in the Spirit on the Sabbath while carrying his stones as he has been doing for years, but this day was different. He heard a voice behind him that sounded like a trumpet. These are John's own words for describing what happened that day.

> "I was in the Spirit on the Lord's Day, and I heard behind me a loud voice, as of a trumpet, saying, "I am the Alpha and the Omega, the First and the Last," and, "What you see, write in a book…" Then I turned to see the voice that spoke with me. And having turned I saw seven golden lampstands, and in the midst of the seven lampstands, One like the Son of Man, clothed with a garment down to the feet and girded about the chest with a golden band. His head and hair were white like wool, as white as snow, and His eyes like a flame of fire; His feet were like fine brass, as if refined in a furnace, and His voice as the sound of

> many waters; He had in His right hand seven stars, out of His mouth went a sharp two-edged sword, and His countenance was like the sun shining in its strength. And when I saw Him, I fell at His feet as dead. But He laid His right hand on me, saying to me, "Do not be afraid; I am the First and the Last. I am He who lives, and was dead, and behold, I am alive forevermore. Amen. And I have the keys of Hades and of Death. Write the things which you have seen, and the things which are, and the things which will take place after this."
>
> – Revelation 1:10-19 NKJV

Take place after this? After what? This is where the tour of heaven begins.

Are you ready for the great adventure? Let's get started!

CHAPTER 2

The Open Door

In Revelation 4, an opened door appeared and John was instructed to walk through it, so he did. And just like that, he was in heaven. No lines, no questions, no interrogation to see if he was good enough, he just walked through a door and there he was.

The first place he was taken by his angel guide was the throne room. That's the only place the prophets had had access to, so perhaps that is always the beginning of the tour. John was amazed at what he saw and gave us much more information than was seen through the peephole of the prophets.

First, John describes a tangible, visible form of God. He says that the appearance of God in spirit form is red, yellow and green lights that form a perfect round circle. He calls it a rainbow, except that it's not an arch, it's a full circle. Around the throne are the seats of the Elders, twenty-four in all; twelve for the tribes of Israel and twelve for the apostles who were over the gentile world and church.

There is a sea of glass before the throne and seraphim who praise God without ceasing. At the time John is in the room, there is some sort of celebration taking place. We don't know if God had sent a blessing, victory or created a new planet, but verse nine reads, ***Whenever the living creatures give glory and honor and thanks to Him who sits on the throne,*** the elders fall off their thrones and throw their crowns at the feet of God. I am sure this was a special occasion, since they had to put their crowns back on in order to do it again ***whenever***. Who knows? Maybe one day we can ask.

As you get into chapter five of John's book that we now call his Revelation, you will see more of his tour. I know the Scriptures tell us that eyes have not, seen, ears have not heard, neither has is even entered into the thoughts and heart of man, the things God has prepared, but I gotta be honest, what John saw next, blows me away. He was taken to a section of the throne room where he witnessed an animal choir. You don't believe me? Read verse 13. John is very specific to tell us who is in the choir. He says, *And every creature which is in heaven and on the earth and under the earth and such as are in the sea, and all that are in them, I heard*... Literally, every creature that has ever existed since the beginning of time. Yes, I said, every animal. I know, it's hard to believe, but I'm only telling you what John saw and wrote. That means Jonah's fish, Balaam's donkey and the rooster that crowed when Peter denied Christ. It also means, your dog - Muffy, your horse, the cow you ate for lunch, the sushi you ate for dinner and the deer hanging on the wall (or perhaps in the garage). I know, I know, it's not what we expected, but it's true. All creatures were made to glorify God and they all get to live in heaven and sing in a choir. That cat you kicked at was just letting you know she is a soprano and the moose you shot is a baritone.

You may say, "But animals don't have a soul..." Well I don't know who started that rumor, but you can take up your theological debate with God, (and your dinner) when you get to heaven. I know they were not made in the image of God, but they do have feelings and a mind, which means there is more to them than just a body. They were created to glorify God and since Jesus calls himself a Lamb and a Lion, and calls Satan a serpent and a dragon, who are we to say that animals aren't spiritual?

The animal choir is not the only choir there. John saw a choir so impressive that he wrote about it in Revelation, chapters 4, 5, 7, 14, 15, and 19. He describes this choir as having 10,000 times 10,000 and 1,000s of 1,000s. I have no idea what number 1,000s of 1,000s is, but it's BIG! From his description, it is as though you can hear them singing no matter where you are in heaven. Their song fills the celestial air of heaven with joyful worship. I can only imagine that this choir has octaves and harmonies unknown to the human ear. John just couldn't quit talking about them. He would say, *I saw a golden city, but there was this choir... I saw angels, and there was this choir... I saw gates of pearl, walls of jasper and streets of gold, but you've just gotta hear this choir!*

The angel guiding John also took him into the galaxy so he could see what the city of heaven looked like from a distance. It was then and only then, that he realized he was looking at a city. The city was made of transparent gold, which is clear, in its purest form. All of the buildings were made of this type of clear gold, so it would be like looking at a city made of thick glass. He described the city as having the appearance of a cube, with 12 layers in the cube. It would be like a 12-story high building except the dimension would be so much larger! Each story would be 125 miles tall. Yes, I said, 125 miles, not feet. I know! That's exactly what I thought when I realized it. it's HUGE! The foundation of the city is made up of 12 jeweled layers. What we call jewelry on earth is used as gravel in heaven. Who knew? There are twelve gates in the city, each with a door approximately 216 feet tall. Oh yes, and you can't miss this part - the door for each gate is one pearl. No, I didn't say pearls. I said a single pearl that is 216 feet tall. I know, that's BIG, too! I have a lot of people I want to meet and things I want to see when I get to heaven, and one of them is the oyster that made those twelve pearls. I bet she is the fat lady that hits the high note in heaven's animal choir. I'm just sayin'...

There is no temple in heaven. Think about it. Why would we need one when we are there with the Father and the Son? There are also no lights there, but John tells us that the glory of the Lamb lights up the entire city. Maybe that is why the buildings are clear; every angle of every wall reflects the glistening glory of Jesus and lights every corridor. Wow, I can't wait to see it!

John saw a river that flowed from God's throne and it was lined with the Tree of Life. It didn't say how many trees of Life there were, only that they lined the crystal clear river. Tree of Life? Read on, I'll explain that one in another chapter.

John's tour ends where eternity begins. God will wipe away every tear, and He will sentence Satan and his demon horde to their eternal punishment. God will take away death, pain, sorrow and there will be nothing but love, joy, peace, worship, friendship, community, and life in the eternal kingdom of our Lord.

Oh yeah, before we finish the tour, I need to tell you that God's eternal plan includes renovating the earth. Why? Good question, I had it, too. I believe God made the universe for His pleasure and glory, so here is my theory: In our glorified bodies, we can go anywhere in the universe we want to go. We can jog on the rings of Saturn or camp on Mars and Pluto. Or better yet, explore unseen galaxies, constellations and nebulas. Or, just go to Hawaii and walk in an active volcano, walk the floor of the sea for a few weeks or just chill in Maui on the beach. It's eternity, so there are no time restraints, except for one, the Sabbath.

The Sabbath is an eternal covenant that God established. The Apostle Peter wrote that one day is a thousand years in heaven. So maybe we explore God's vast creation with our loved ones in our glorified body and then on the Sabbath, or every seventh thousand years, we hear the shofars blowing, and the glory of Jesus leads us on the path to the celestial city for a day (one thousand years) of worship and then it all starts over again. Maybe on the Sabbaths we can join the Hallelujah chorus and sing with cherubim and seraphim. Maybe we get to sing with the animal choir, or sing the triumphant song of the redeemed that the angels cannot sing. Ah, just the thought of it, fills my heart with joy and hope!

CHAPTER 3

Eternal Life is a Real Life

WHAT KIND OF eternity will you have? Did that question throw you off a little when you read it? It should have. Many people work under the assumption that eternity is the same for everyone, but that's not what the Bible teaches. Let me explain.

I know that eternity is usually viewed as a time without end. Well, that part will be the same for everyone, but suppose I told you that three different families moved to the same city and lived there for twenty-five years. Do you think they all had the same experiences in that length of time? The answer is obviously no. There are parts of eternity that will be the same for everyone; like spending time with Jesus, being immortal, being in heaven, and so forth. But there is also a part of heaven that will be different for everyone; that part is the rewards and treasures that we have laid up in heaven while living our life on earth. Not exactly a class system, more like an honor system.

Heaven is so much more than sitting on a cloud talking to Moses. It's more than an eternal worship service, even though that part will be amazing. Eternity is a real life! And the status of that life is determined by one thing—your labors for God on this earth. Regardless of whether you were a missionary, a martyr or had a deathbed repentance, when you get to heaven; it's better than the best this world has to offer. Nevertheless, we can't ignore the fact that our labors for God on this earth follow us into eternity.

> Then I heard a voice from heaven saying to me, "Write: 'Blessed are the dead who die in the Lord from now on.'" "Yes," says the Spirit, "that they may rest from their labors, and their works follow them."
>
> – Revelation 14:13

Reading our Bible, paying our tithes, helping the poor, ministering to the hurting, and sharing the gospel is not only a part of our life now, but these works will follow us. Many people have lived sacrificial lives for the cause of God's kingdom and God has a plan to reward them for those sacrifices.

One of the most quoted verses in the Bible is John 3:16. *"For God so loved the world that He gave His only begotten Son, that whoever believes in Him should not perish but have everlasting life."* Everlasting life is a powerful term. First it's…well, everlasting, eternal. Secondly, it's life. A real life, just like life here, except it's celestial and immortal life instead of everyday mortality. The Scriptures use the phrase 'eternal life' 32 times (NKJV). John 10:28 reads, *"And I give them eternal life, and they shall never perish; neither shall anyone snatch them out of My hand."* Romans 6:23 reads, *"For the wages of sin is death, but the gift of God is eternal life in Christ Jesus our Lord."*

Heaven is filled with routines, places to go, people to see, and with purpose. I believe Heaven has planned trips, guided tours, story-telling rooms, libraries, animals, banquets to attend, ceremonies, galaxy tours, and that we can even come back to the recreated earth to visit or stay for a while (*see* Revelation 21:1). What if there are houses, neighborhoods, tea parties, birthday parties, and having friends over for dinner? That is not too far-fetched for me. The Bible records angels eating, socializing, ascending up and down ladders, riding horses, warring, reading scrolls, giving guided tours, and much more. It doesn't sound like the angel world is sitting around humming hymns. You can certainly do that if you want, but after that, an eternal adventure awaits, a real life.

Eternal Life is a Real Life

Wow! It sounds like eternity has everything. Well, actually not everything. It doesn't have a jail; it doesn't have a hospital; it doesn't have taxes; it doesn't have an election. It doesn't have tears; it doesn't have pain; it doesn't even have a sun. It doesn't have a nursing home; it doesn't have a graveyard; and it doesn't have a war zone. It doesn't have a rehab center; it doesn't have a counseling office; and guess what, it doesn't even have a church. There's not one church *building* in the new Jerusalem, you won't need one then.

The first thing that happens to prepare you for eternity is your new body. Not just a new body – but a glorified, immortal body. The Bible states there are terrestrial bodies and celestial bodies (*1 Corinthians 15:40*). Terrestrial bodies are the ones we have on the earth. Celestial bodies are heavenly bodies, like the bodies of the angels. Just think about it for a moment. Angels have walked through walls, walked in fiery furnaces, descended from heaven to earth, and ascended back. They can fly, they can eat, they can ride, and they can communicate. There's no gym for that kind of workout. It's God's gift so that we can enjoy an eternal life without restraint or limitation. This new body doesn't break down, it doesn't age, and it needs no sleep to rejuvenate. 1st Corinthians 15:50-53 says that we get the body in an instant, ***in the twinkling of an eye, at the last trumpet.*** No surgery, just instantaneous.

These bodies do not all look alike. If God took the time to uniquely design every human being who has ever lived with different fingerprints and made sure that we understand every snowflake is different, every tree is different, every flower is different and every animal is different, then why would we think our celestial bodies will be cloned? He has fashioned your celestial body just for you, so that you can be recognized and appreciated for who you were on the earth. All of the celestial bodies mentioned in the Bible have wings. The cherubim, seraphim and archangels are all mentioned with wings. Even the unnamed angels in the books of Daniel and Revelation have wings. Wings may be standard protocol for celestial bodies. Personally, I hope so. I can't wait to fly!

Philippians 3:20-21 reads, *For our citizenship is in heaven, from which we also eagerly wait for the Savior, the Lord Jesus Christ, who will transform our lowly body that it may be conformed to His glorious body*... So the closest picture we have to a glorious form is the Mount of Transfiguration. Matthew 17:1-2, Mark 9:2-3, Luke 9:29 – these Scriptures all say He was whiter than white (so to speak), but they don't say He was transparent. He also had a face that glowed like the sun. That may not be the permanent glorified body, but that was certainly the part of glorification Jesus allowed them to see.

What we do know is that our bodies in heaven will be a brand new breed of celestial creature that will be distinguished and unique. When you walk through heaven, you will say, "There's Michael, he's an archangel. There's an angel of the seraphim, 'Hi, Raphael.' Oh! Here comes a glorified son or daughter of God."

God has something special for us. Not only do we get a new body, but God is also going to make a new earth, too. He is going to do away with anything toxic, everything that is harmful, and He is going to recreate everything free from the contaminants of sin. Isaiah 65:17 reads, *For behold, I create new heavens and a new earth; And the former shall not be remembered or come to mind.* And in Isaiah 66:22, *"For as the new heavens and the new earth which I will make shall remain before Me", says the Lord.* Wow, that's powerful! God's going to make new heavens and a new earth and they will never fade from Him.

The Apostle John wrote in the Book of Revelation, *"Now I saw a new heaven and a new earth, for the first heaven and the first earth had passed away. Also there was no more sea."* (21:1) We have already talked about the animal choir in heaven, so I guess there is no need for a sea anymore. Who knows, maybe pigs will fly, as well as whales, dolphins and trout.

Have you ever seen a Thomas Kincaid painting? Besides being the Painter of Light™, one of the things that makes Kincaid paintings so unique is that he paints flowers out of their season. If you know anything about plants, you can see he puts plants together that do not bloom at the same time. When you see a Kincaid, you'll see snow and then you will see plants blooming that should not be blooming in the snow. You will see all of the seasons coming together. Remember his famous painting entitled, "Gate to Heaven"? It shows spring, summer and autumn plants in full color and all at the same time.

I believe that is how God is going to recreate the earth. There will be no seasons, because Revelation says there will be no sun. I believe it is one eternal season and all the seasons and the beauty of those seasons will come together.

Imagine with me—I am in this beautiful place enjoying all of the four seasons at once. My wife, Faith, and I, and our family are looking at all the incredible flowers God made and I am walking down the creek and I see the laurel and the magnolias. I see the azaleas in full bloom. I am breathing in this incredible air and it is like this moment that I never want to fade away. Let's say we've been on the flower tour for about ten years and then decide we would like to explore more of God's creation, so we all decide to fly to Jupiter to explore canyons and rock formations. Heaven is not just songs and stories, it's a real life!

It's a lot to digest, dare you keep on reading?

CHAPTER 4

The Garment of Praise

Heaven sparkles with light! It dances off every corner of the transparent city. It glistens from the foundations and reflects light beams through every wall. It bursts with a kaleidoscope of colors and fills the sky with a thousand rainbows. We need no lights there because it is a city of light—the light of the Lamb.

When God describes Himself in a tangible form, He only uses two descriptions: light and fire. In two other places, the Bible tells us God is love and God is Spirit. Other than the names of God, these are the only descriptions He gives about Himself. Since we can't see breath or love, we can only see God in the colors of light and fire. When John was taking his tour of heaven, he saw the throne of God and said the One who sat on the throne was made up of three colors: red, amber and green. He described the view as a tri-colored circle or a round rainbow. The light emanated and illuminated heaven. Then he told us that we will have no need of the sun or any source of light in the city of New Jerusalem because the glory of God and the Lamb will be its light. Okay, I'm getting chills, just thinking about it.

John's Revelation also says that when the Bride of Christ is presented, she is wearing a new garment arrayed with every precious jewel. Can you imagine a diamond dress that is beaded with sapphires, emeralds, opals, rubies, and amethysts? This garment is obviously worn to make the Bride beautiful, but that is not its only purpose. This is the garment of praise. It was worn long before mankind was created.

Heaven on My Mind

The original diamond gown was worn by the archangel, Lucifer, who was created to reflect the glory of God.

Let me explain! The angel Lucifer is the one who failed and became Satan, the enemy of God. But before that, he was the one who stood before God's throne in the garment of praise and produced music. The description of Lucifer is found in two places in the Bible: Isaiah 14 and Ezekiel 28. In Isaiah, it says that he was created with stringed instruments inside of him. In Ezekiel, it says that he also had percussion instruments (timbrels) and pipes, or wind instruments. It's intriguing to me that every instrument in the world is classified in these three categories: percussion, wind and strings. It appears that these unique abilities allowed Lucifer to create any genre of music he chose and his musical ability was so supernatural that it filled the atmosphere of heaven with sound and inspiration. When he led worship, he stood before the throne of God, but was required to wear the garment of praise. Ezekiel 28:13 states that "every precious stone" was his covering.

I want you to see this heavenly scene. Lucifer is called upon to lead worship, so he drapes himself in the garment of praise and comes before the throne of God to create mind-blowing, supernatural musical rhythms and melodies. Because he is in front of the throne, the garment of praise reflects the light of God all throughout heaven and literally makes Lucifer invisible to the eye. He is there, but the garment reflects the glory of God so much that he becomes a light bearer. That is actually, what the word Lucifer means, "light bearer."

The closest thing we have to that would be a disco ball. When a single ray of light hits a twirling disco ball, it reflects millions of light beams all around the room and turns a dark room into a wonderland of starlight. Now multiply that by a million and you will see a twirling angel dressed with every precious stone, which means it is multi-colored and it's shimmering the colors of red, amber and green into the universe. The scene is brilliantly magnificent! Exhale now! Just give me a minute…alright, I'm good now, but I'll never view worship the same way again.

The garment of praise makes the wearer of the garment invisible to others because all they can see is the magnification of God's glory emanating from them. This spinning angel with unlimited musical abilities was heaven's worship leader. The invisibility of Lucifer became his prideful downfall. He knew how talented he was, but he wanted to be seen. That is why in Isaiah 14, he said, *I will exalt myself, sit on the mountain of God, ascend above the clouds and be like the Most High God.* He didn't just want to reflect God's glory; he wanted to take some of the glory for himself because of his talent. Pride became his demise.

Lucifer was banished and became Satan, but the garment of praise remained and is worn by God's people every time they worship. And one day, it will be worn by the Bride of Christ. When God made man, He created in him the same abilities for worship that He created in Lucifer. You have within yourself all three categories of musical instruments. In order for you to praise God, you have to blow air through your pipes, we call it a windpipe. The air passes through your strings, we call them cords or vocal cords. Musical notes are also called chords. Once you produce the sound of praise with the first two instruments you add the final touch and clap your hands to create percussion and rhythms. You, too, are a finely-tuned instrument of praise. When you truly go before God with the garment of praise on, you become invisible to the eyes of others and only reflect the glory of God. In other words, they see God in you, but not you. When we make worship about ourselves, our preferences, our genres, our talents, we essentially take on the prideful nature of Lucifer. But when we worship to glorify God and not to be seen, we take on the nature of the Bride. We become the spinning, twirling being that reflects the light of God's glory.

When an eagle flies, he is majestic and we can't take our eyes off him. But when pursued by an enemy, the eagle will fly toward the sun. The light of the sun begins to blind the eyes of his predator. The closer he gets to the sun, the more the eagle becomes invisible, and all the predator can see is the blinding light of the sun. So it is with us and worship. When pursued by our enemy, we run to the Light. We veil ourselves in the garment of praise and the closer we get to the light of God's glory, the more invisible we become. **"Oh, magnify the Lord with me, and let us exalt His name together."** (Psalm 34:3)

CHAPTER 5

Fourteen Things that God Records and Rewards

THE LONG-AWAITED DAY finally arrives! It's payday! Now we get to see how much eternal currency we have to spend. Oh! Didn't you know? You have been laying up treasures in heaven *(Matthew 6)*. What did you think they were for? Well, since we don't get them until our life is over, I can only assume that we will get to use them in eternity. That's right. I believe we have a storehouse in heaven with our treasure in it.

Some call it the Bema Judgement Seat of Christ and others refer to it as the Coronation Day. The title you give it is unimportant. What is important is you realize that all of your deeds have been recorded and will one day be rewarded. That's right. An angel has been following you around writing your kingdom biography. For instance,

October

Monday—gave a cup of water to the man cutting the lawn.

Tuesday—had a life group meeting at their house.

Wednesday—was kind to the new employee learning the cash register.

Thursday—prayed for 30 minutes.

Friday—gave the struggling waitress an extra tip.

Saturday—shared their faith with a neighbor

Sunday—worshipped, prayed and rested. (Obeyed a commandment)

Monday—didn't snap back when boss was angry.

Tuesday—loved on family and told a Bible story.

Wednesday—gave away their favorite coat to a cold man.

Thursday—submitted to authority even though the boss was wrong.

Friday—wrote out their tithe check to the church.

Saturday—had a single mother over to dinner.

Raphael, GUARDIAN TO (INSERT YOUR NAME)

Your guardian angel is doing much more than pushing you out of the way of oncoming traffic. He is also assigned to record your deeds. He follows you closely with pad in hand, perhaps a calculator, and if he's over 40, maybe a pair of eyeglasses hanging on the end of his nose. Okay, not the eyeglasses, since we do have a glorified body, but, I'm pretty sure the rest of it is accurate. The scene for "payday" is set for us in the Book of Revelation, chapter 20.

> "And I saw the dead, small and great, standing before God, and books were opened. And another book was opened, which is the Book of Life. And the dead were judged according to their works, by the things which were written in the books."
>
> – REVELATION 20:12

Pay careful attention to the language of this verse. First, books were opened; then another book, the Book of Life. Since we can only speculate on the Book of Life, let me take my stab at it. I think there is a Book of Life for every person who lives. I think it is the book of *your* Life, as God sees you. I believe your sins have been blotted out and it only records your good works in God's kingdom and that is why this book is opened on the day you stand before God. I have many reasons for coming to this conclusion, but that is another chapter for a different book.

Fourteen Things that God Records and Rewards

Matthew 16:27 says, **For the Son of Man will come in the glory of His Father with His angels, and then He will reward each according to his works.** In the parable of the talents, the Parable of the Minas, and the Good Samaritan parable, there is always a reward when "HE" returns. Ok, so now we all believe that there is a reward for our work, but a huge question still remains, "What do we get rewarded for?"

Here is the short list and their scriptural references:

1. Your labor of love to other Christians *(Hebrews 6:10-11)*
2. Charitable deeds done in secret *(Matthew 6:1-4)*
3. Opening your home to others *(Matthew 10:40-42)*
4. Any act of kindness *(Mark 9:41)*
5. Keeping the commandments *(Revelation 14:12-13)*
6. Living with Integrity *(Psalm 18:20)*
7. Doing good things with a pure motive *(Jeremiah 17:10)*
8. Preaching willingly, not just for money *(1ˢᵗ Corinthians 9:16-17)*
9. The words we speak ('Points' deducted for speaking death; 'points' rewarded for speaking life.) *(Matthew 12:36-37)*
10. Evangelism/leading people to Christ *(1ˢᵗ Thessalonians 2:19-20)*
11. Lending to those who cannot pay you back *(Luke 6:35-36)*
12. Being kind to an enemy *(Proverbs 25:21-22)*
13. Prayer *(Matthew 6:6)*
14. Submitting to others *(Colossians 3:17-24)*

We are not exactly sure what we will receive for these deeds, but one thing is sure, these deeds are all recorded and rewarded. The simplest act of kindness gets noticed and noted in heaven. One day, we will all be surprised when we read our kingdom biography. I am certain that many of the things we thought would be in it will not even be there and most of the things written about us in the book, we will not even remember doing, because our motives were selfless and pure. If heaven has a family album, you and I will one day turn to a picture page of ourselves in some of our most humble and unflattering moments. And on that page, you will see the smudge on your cheeks, a dust rag in your hand and a smile on your Father's face. Beside the photo could even be a caption bubble outside the Father's smile that reads, "Well done."

CHAPTER 6

When God Made Adam and Eve, They Lived Naked! Are You Worried?

When we're invited someplace really special, we always ask, "What should I wear?" don't we? So, what will we wear in heaven?

I know when God made Adam and Eve, they didn't wear clothes. The thought of that is a little frightening for those of us in this day and time. Of course, they didn't mind; they were married, and were the only two people on the planet. Remember, it was for Adam and Eve that God designed the first garments and covered them. From that time forward, He has not only required clothing, but has used clothing and colors to signify rank, status and identification of people.

He required the priests to wear certain clothing, and the High Priest to wear totally different apparel. Even Royalty dressed differently so they could easily be identified as the king or queen. According to Scripture, angels were always clothed.

In heaven, it doesn't appear that clothing is given for covering as much as it is for identification. What you wear indicates who you are—or perhaps we should say—who you were on the earth.

There are many classifications of citizenship mentioned in the heaven, and each dresses according to their eternal status. The Bible mentions saints. I can only assume that means everyone who goes to heaven - you know, like the song, "Oh when the saints go marching in." I'm not sure if there is a march (I don't remember reading about it), but I do know that saints arrive in heaven every day, possibly even every second of the day. In the book of Revelation, we are told that all the tribulation saints are issued white robes upon arrival to heaven. I don't know what other colors there will be.

I think there must be an orientation upon arrival which includes the welcome, the tour, and resident assignment. I doubt you are given a key to your house, since no thieves are allowed there and every visitor is a welcomed pleasure. I assume that orientation explains the garment system of heaven that may go something like this, "In heaven there are only five crowns. This is what each looks like and this is what they mean." (Chapter 8 is about these five crowns, so I won't elaborate here.) Perhaps the angels continue with, "If you see someone wearing purple, they are royalty. They will rule on the earth during the Lord's millennium as a king. Their sash will identify the country, state, or city they will rule over. If you see red, they have an eternal priestly status and will serve in that region as one of God's priests. Oh, and don't forget the halos."

Halos are crowns of glory that never fade away. Crowns of glory are given to those who lived a righteous life on the earth; meaning they lived their life through the righteousness of Christ and strived daily to be Christ-like in their character. In Hebrew, 'glory' means 'light', thus it is a circle of light over their head.

So yes, for those who thought they would have to give up their favorite sport of mall sprinting, shopping may be necessary.

Since clothing is important to God, and colors signify ranks, and ceremonial robes are required, we can only assume there must be lots of other clothing in heaven in the category of *"Eye has not seen, nor ear heard, Nor have entered into the heart of man, the things which God has prepared for those who love Him."* (1st Corinthians 2:9)

It's obvious that heaven is a place of fashion and style. The crown of glory alone is a glowing halo over a person's head. I'd call that styling. How about the jewels mentioned in the garments? Isaiah 61 talks about garments of salvation and jewelry worn by brides and bridegrooms. If heaven is a place of many rooms, I am certain there is a clothing room or perhaps something equivalent to a mall on the earth.

Think about where and to what events various garments could be worn in heaven. Suppose you were going to walk by the River of Life and pick fruit from the trees. What if you were going swimming in the sea of glass or perhaps heading to a banquet to honor someone's ministry on the earth? There is worship attire, ceremonial attire, leisure attire, and since we don't sleep in heaven, why would we need a mansion, except to entertain guests and house personal belongings, like clothing perhaps? It's just a theory, but it can be argued apologetically with scriptures.

CHAPTER 7

Heaven is a Real Place, Not Life on a Cloud

In My Father's house are many mansions; if it were not so, I would have told you. I go to prepare a place for you. And if I go and prepare a place for you, I will come again and receive you to Myself; that where I am, there you may be also.

– JOHN 14:2-3

WHAT DO YOU think about when you think about life in heaven? Sitting on clouds, talking to Bible characters and playing harps? Playing harps and eating angel food cake? For real? Give me a break! Who started that rumor?

Heaven is a real place. Finis Jennings Dake, a great Bible theologian, refers to it as the 'planet heaven'. I'm not sure if it's actually a planet, but if it helps you think of it in real terms, then "planet heaven" works just fine.

The Bible is very clear to let us know the location of heaven. It's in the farthest sides of North, above the North Star in an empty part of the universe. Job 26:7 tells us, **"He stretched out the north over an empty place..."** Psalm 75:6 reads, **"For promotion comes neither from the east, nor from the west, nor from the south..."** Ezekiel 1:4, **"And I looked and, behold, a whirlwind was coming out of the north..."** Lucifer who wanted to sit on God's throne declared in Isaiah 14:13, **"I will ascend** *into heaven, I will exalt my throne above the stars of God; I will also sit on the mount of the congregation on the farthest sides of the north."*

GLIMPSES OF HEAVEN

There are men who were given glimpses of heaven and each one gives us some insight into its untold treasures. Abraham looked for a city not made by hands, but one that had foundations whose builder and maker was God *(Hebrews 11:9-11)*. John the Baptist saw the heavens open at Jesus' baptism and saw a dove and heard a voice (Matthew 3:16-17). Peter saw heavens open in Acts 10 and God said, "Eat." (Some of you got real excited when you read that, didn't you? Can you imagine angel-baked lasagna and homemade ice cream from a heavenly cow?) Stephen saw the heavens open in Acts 7 and saw Jesus standing at the right hand of the Father. Ezekiel saw the heavens opened and saw horses and chariots. In Revelation 4, John saw thrones and white robes and crowns of gold, lamps of fire, lightning and thunder, books, and much more.

WHAT IS HEAVEN LIKE?

John 14 – mansions in heaven

Revelation 4 – thrones, seats, lamps

Daniel 7 & 9 – books in heaven

Revelation 8 – doors, coals of fire and altars

Revelation 9 – trumpets and golden bowls

Hebrews 8 – a sea of glass, rainbows

Revelation Chapters 4 & 5 – fountains and rivers of crystal clear water

Revelation 4, 5, 7, 14, 15, & 19 – singing and worship and lots of musical instruments

Food is mentioned many times. Manna is mentioned as angels' food in Exodus 16, and fruit is mentioned in Revelation 22. In Luke 22:30, Jesus refers to eating and drinking at His table.

Horses in heaven are mentioned multiple times. Saddle up, boys!

The Bible mentions all of the following tangible things in heaven: chairs, chariots, thrones, books, fire, rainbows, river, trees, mountains, sea, golden bowls, altars, and every animal that has ever existed. Yes, even the T-Rex and the (dinosaur)! It mentions jewels and jewelry, crowns, candles and robes. It talks about libraries and banquet rooms. It mentions everyday activities like eating, talking, walking, singing, worshipping, sitting, standing, and if you take the river in Ezekiel 47 as a literal river in heaven, then even swimming is mentioned.

Heaven has lots of nature and horticulture; growing trees with fruit on them, mountains, rainbows, and even flowing rivers! It mentions flowers, lights, stars, and fragrances. Remember, God did put Adam in a garden when He created him.

When I was a kid, my parents listened to a lot of Southern Gospel music. I remember one fun song that was sung by Jake Hess and the Imperials, called the First Day in Heaven. It was a fast, hand-clapping, foot-stomping and (in my church) high-jumping song. It went something like this:

> "Well it's a great, great morning, your first day in Heaven, when you stroll down the golden avenue. There are mansions left and right and you're thrilled at every sight, and the saints are always smiling, saying "How do you do?" Oh it's a great, great morning, your first day in Heaven, when you realize your worrying days are through. You'll be glad you were not idle, took time to read your Bible, it's a great morning for you." [2]

It kind of has a nice ring to it, doesn't it? Not too deep theologically, but certainly a catchy tune that you will find yourself singing all throughout the day.

How Much Can You Imagine?

> "Eye has not seen, nor ear heard,
> neither have entered into the heart of men
> the things which God hath prepared for them that love Him."
> — 1ˢᵗ Corinthians 2:9

Since heaven is bigger than your imagination, go ahead and let your creativity flow. As I write this, I am flying over cloud cover somewhere between Detroit, Michigan and Richmond, Virginia. The sun is beginning to set and I can see at least ten colors in the horizon. Since it's time to imagine, I would love to just take out flying through those colors. I'm not talking about in the airplane; I'm talking about in the plain air. It would be fun. Or maybe I could ride a flying horse like the one in Revelation 18 and we could ride to the end of that sunset. I don't know if it will be exactly like that or not, but one thing I do know, it far surpasses my wildest dreams and imaginations.

CHAPTER 8

The Five Crowns Worn in Heaven

I'VE GOT TO admit, the idea of wearing a crown sounds uncomfortable at first. Just think about it, all that gold sitting balanced on top of your head. Is it heavy? I can almost see a nun-like angel with a stick poking me in the back, saying, "Straighten up or your crown will fall off." Do we have crown boxes similar to hat boxes where we store them if we want to take a swim or something? Do we have to get them shined at the crown shinery? Hey, I'm just sayin'. I've never owned a crown or knew anyone who did, unless you count the tiaras worn by the little girls in my house. I've always heard people say things like, "You've just earned another jewel in your crown." I've even heard them say, "God will put a star in your crown for that good deed." A star? Is there Scripture reference for that? Are we talking real stars or star shapes? It is heaven, so I guess anything is possible. I'm sure the subject of crowns in heaven interests you, too, so let's talk about it. Want more? Okay, fasten your seat belt. This is going to be a wild ride.

Before we go any further, you might want to know that you can get a crown and lose it before you get to heaven. I know you just said out loud, "What? He's nuts!" Don't worry, the thought occurred to me, too, when I discovered it. Revelation 3:11 says, *"Behold, I am coming quickly! Hold fast what you have, that no one may take your crown."* Some of you are going to read this and realize it was written to the church of Philadelphia and assume it only applies to people who live in Philly. That would be a wrong assumption. You have to realize that all of these crowns are given at the end of the race. All of them are like trophies for finishing well. So even though the race may not always be to the swift, you want to finish well and obtain your crown!

You might want to sit down for this one. Are you sitting? Okay, here it is. In heaven, some people will wear crowns and others may not. Shocking? Crowns are earned for actions done here on earth. There are only five crowns referenced in Scripture, and each one is given for a particular reason. I know you are curious about them, so let's get right to it.

As I said, the Bible only mentions five crowns in heaven. Before you read the list, keep in mind this in no way implies that there are only five. There could be many the Bible doesn't mention. These crowns were never given in a listing together, but rather mentioned randomly by various Bible writers. Remember, eyes have not seen nor ears heard the things God has in store for us. However, the understanding of these five which are mentioned gives great insight to the purpose for wearing crowns in heaven.

Here are the five that are mentioned:

- Crown of Righteousness – given to those who finish

- Crown of Endurance – given to those who are disciplined

- Crown of Life – given to martyrs, both dead and alive

- Crown of Glory – given to Shepherds who cared unselfishly for others

- Crown of Rejoicing – given to soul winners

Let's start with the crown of righteousness. Since we really don't know who is truly righteous in the sight of God, I think we may be surprised when this crown is given. Some who think they deserve it may not get it at all and others who humbly served in obscurity may receive it as those of us from the earth hear the name of an unknown person who was heroically famous in heaven. It will come as no surprise to the angels, but we may say, "Who is that?" The Apostle Paul mentions this crown in 2nd Timothy 4:6-8. It is the first and only time he mentions it. He chooses to wait until the time of his death to talk about it and indicates that it will be given because he fought a good fight, kept the faith and finished the race. It would seem that this is a crown for those who "finish" their assignments. We have all wanted to quit, and I can think of no one who had a better reason than the Apostle Paul, but perhaps during one of the angelic visits he received, this information was passed on to him. He chose to reveal it at the end of his race, when he had earned enough credit through tribulations to authenticate it. Many have fought a good fight but didn't keep the faith. Those who kept the faith finished the race. I think keeping faith is the key to completing your assignment. If you lose heart, you will quit for all the wrong reasons. Remember who called you, remember who you serve and remember the crown.

While the crown of righteousness is for finishing, the Apostle Paul mentions another crown for those who endure. He calls this an imperishable crown. This crown does not carry the same title, but has similarities in that it is also given to those who finish the race. He calls it the prize. He mentions the fight again but doesn't talk about the end of the race, but rather the middle of it. One phrase seems to sum up the reason for this crown. He says, "I discipline my body and bring it into subjection."

Living a disciplined life is a choice. Undisciplined living is also a choice. One is obviously easier than the other because one chooses temporary indulgences over eternal ones. Discipline requires routine and repetition to be successful. You can't just try to make a good choice in the moment or you will hit and miss your way through life. It's more about working to develop a Christ-like character than trying to do good things. A good character will cause you to do good things and make wise choices. The discipline of a disciple is about finding a daily routine that develops you a little more each day into the image of Christ. Think of an athlete or a body builder. They can't just play when they feel like it. A daily discipline conditions them for moments of battle and competition. Our daily routine as a Christian conditions us for the showdown with the enemy that will come in moments of temptation. We win in those moments because we have been growing stronger every day. The crown of endurance is given to those who have lived disciplined lives. And as we all know, it's easier said than done—so get started.

Next is the crown of life. It was promised to the Smyrna church in Revelation 2:8-11. The Smyrna church represents an era of the church where suffering and persecution were necessary to profess Christianity. It seems ironic that in much of the world, suffering Christianity is frowned upon. Most people just want a feel-good gospel and an express lane church experience on the weekend that doesn't take up too much of their time. We look more like the Laodicean church which is more about money and refineries that the Smyrna church that endured the refiner's fire. This church experienced poverty, suffering, imprisonment, and death, yet remained faithful.

James, the brother of our Lord, also mentions this particular crown in the book of the Bible that bears his name. The crown of life is given to Christian martyrs. Not just those who died, but those who lived through hell on earth to keep the gospel alive. Our definition for martyrs is too narrow. It's not just a person who died; it's a person who gave up life, but perhaps lived many more years in a state of suffering for the gospel's sake. I know a pastor in Vietnam who has been imprisoned 18 times for preaching the gospel. No, I didn't read about him in Foxes' Book of Martyrs.[3] I know this man. I have eaten a meal with him. He has spent as long as three years in a hard labor camp for preaching. He is still preaching today in that country and he is still faithful. He keeps a prison bag with him at all times because he knows that is the price for preaching in his country, yet he continues. He will wear this crown and will be honored all throughout eternity as one of heaven's kings because of the life of suffering he has lived on this earth. No one signs up for this, but those who are called to it will have an eternal status of elite-ness, because the first will be last and the last will be first in heaven.

I am particularly fond of this next crown because I am a pastor. Apostle Peter calls it the crown of glory and it's promised to those who were the caretakers of God's sheep, the Shepherds. It is actually in writing to the elders of the church in 1st Peter 5:1-4 that he mentions it. He exhorts them to shepherd the flock of God under their care and to do it with pure, unselfish motives and to not try to control people, then God will give them a crown of glory. There is nothing more emotionally and mentally draining than caring for other people. While it is fulfilling, it also takes a big dose of selflessness to keep doing it. It feels good when people appreciate it and you can see them growing. However, when extra grace is required to see them through long illnesses, devastating crisis, life-altering disappointments, deaths, disease, and the struggles of life, it can get very exhausting. Many do not last, but those who do are crowned.

One thing that every crown in heaven has in common is endurance and finishing. No one receives a crown unless they finish the race. Keep going, Shepherds! Long hours—keep going. Unappreciated—keep your eye on the prize and keep going. Misunderstood—keep going. Worn out—rest, but keep going. Burn out—get counseling, but keep going. Taken advantage of—remember who you serve—and keep going. Lonely? Forgotten? Forsaken? Rejected? We all understand and you are not alone—just keep going! Betrayed by friends—overlooked by leaders—hated by some—it is part of the calling. Rejoice—and KEEP GOING!

The Apostle Paul also mentions a crown of rejoicing. It is given to soul winners. Listen to how he writes about it in 1st Thessalonians 2:19-20, *"For what is our hope, or joy, or crown of rejoicing? Is it not even you in the presence of our Lord Jesus Christ at His coming? For you are our glory and joy."* Of all the things we do for God, nothing is more important than sharing our faith and winning others to the Lord; anything less is just selfishness. Did that sting? Sorry, but it's still true. We can't just find Jesus and keep Him all to ourselves, asking Him to thrill us "one more time" because it's Sunday. Somewhere along the way, many have reduced the King of all kings to songs, sermons and services. What a shame! We are the light of the world and we cannot hide the light. Jesus moves into the neighborhood when you do. Our daily desire should be to share our faith before the day is over and sadly, some haven't done that in years and still others have never done it. This crown is given only to those who win souls, evangelize, share their faith, or whatever you've come to call it in your tribe.

As I write this chapter, I am sitting in Cambodia and it's 3:30am. My body thinks it's 2:30pm in St. Louis and I can't get my body clock to understand that we are on the other side of the planet. So what do you do? I prayed, then read, but can't read too well when I'm tired, so I did what I never do on a trip, I turned on the TV. The only thing that wasn't Chinese or Cambodian was the Winter Olympics. I watched for a while and it inspired me to turn on the lights and write this chapter on crowns.

The closest thing I can think of to Coronation Day in heaven is the Olympic Ceremony where we place gold medallions around the winners' necks while placing them high on a pedestal for all the world to see. The announcer calls their name, they stand before the masses and walk up on the pedestal to have the gold, silver or bronze medals placed around their necks. The nations are watching and all we see is one person, many times from another country, but in that moment, we all know who they are, what they did and we all know their name. However, those who finish 4th are rarely remembered. As a matter of fact, many Olympians are forgotten, but the names of the gold winners remain a part of our history forever. They finished well.

The closest record in the Bible to a heavenly Coronation Day is found in Daniel 7. I actually believe this is a window into heaven on the day Jesus was crowned as King of kings. I believe this actually happened during the 3 days that Jesus was in the grave and ascended into heaven. Just read **Daniel 7:9-14** and you can decide for yourself.

> *⁹ I watched till **thrones were put in place**,*
>   ***And the Ancient of Days was seated; (The Father)***
>   *His garment was white as snow, And the hair of His head was like pure wool.*
>   *His throne was a fiery flame, Its wheels a burning fire;*

The Five Crowns Worn in Heaven

¹⁰ *A fiery stream issued, And came forth from before Him.*
A thousand thousands ministered to Him;
Ten thousand times ten thousand stood before Him.
<u>The court was seated, And the books were opened.</u>

¹¹ *I watched then because of the sound of the pompous words which the horn was speaking; I watched till* **<u>the beast was slain</u>**, *and its body destroyed and given to the burning flame.* **(Satan defeated)**

¹² *As for the rest of the beasts,* **<u>they had their dominion taken away</u>**, *yet their lives were prolonged for a season and a time.* **(demons)**

¹³ *I was watching in the night visions, And behold,*
<u>One like the Son of Man, Coming with the clouds of heaven</u>! **(Jesus ascending)**
<u>He came to the Ancient of Days,</u> *And they brought Him near before Him.*

¹⁴ *Then* **<u>to Him was given dominion and glory and a kingdom,</u>** *That all peoples, nations, and languages should serve Him.*
His dominion is an everlasting dominion, Which shall not pass away, And His kingdom the one Which shall not be destroyed.

I've got cold chills!

CHAPTER 9

No Lost Tears

*You <u>number my wanderings</u>; Put
<u>my tears</u> into <u>Your bottle</u>;
Are they not in <u>Your book</u>?*

— PSALM 56:8

THIS PASSAGE REPRESENTS millions who have wandered. Wandering speaks of losing your way, or just losing sight of the path. Wanderers pray desperate prayers, they worship extravagantly, they pray without ceasing, and they cry bitterly before God. Many preachers today only want to offer a feel-good message that says nothing bad is going to happen to you if you "stay tuned in to this channel and stick with me as your guide." Yet, all of us know the greatest giants in the Kingdom of God are men with battle scars and chinks in their armor. Most of us as God's children have walked through seasons of faith where we feel nothing, see nothing and it looks like our enemy has the upper hand. That is where we learn to deepen our trust in God. That is where we lean on Lamentations 3 and declare, "Great is His faithfulness and His mercies are renewed every day." We have all asked the question of God, "Why me? Why this? Why now? Why this way? Why? Why? Why?" Some people will try to shame you for saying such things, but secretly in their heart, they have had the same questions. It's the plight of the wanderer. If God can number our wanderings, put our tears in a bottle and write about those days in His book, then why doesn't He do something about our painful plight? If we didn't have seasons like this, we would have no tears in a bottle, and that is something you want to have when you get to heaven. Let me explain.

The Great Hall of Faith

Hebrews 11 records the pain of the Kingdom. Keep in mind, this Hall of Faith is heaven's trophy, not hell's. It's God's victories, not Satan's. As you read this, just imagine the scars of the cloud of witnesses cheering you on from heaven's grandstands. *(Hebrews 12:1)*

> "Who through faith subdued kingdoms, worked righteousness, obtained promises, stopped the mouths of lions, quenched the violence of fire, escaped the edge of the sword, out of weakness were made strong, became valiant in battle, turned to flight the armies of the aliens. Women received their dead raised to life again. And others were tortured, not accepting deliverance, that they might obtain a better resurrection. Still others had trial of mockings and scourgings, yes, and of chains and imprisonment. They were stoned, they were sawn in two, were tempted, were slain with the sword. They wandered about in sheepskins and goatskins, being destitute, afflicted, tormented— of whom the world was not worthy. They wandered in deserts and mountains, in dens and caves of the earth, And all these, having obtained a good testimony through faith, did not receive the promise, God having provided something better for us, that they should not be made perfect apart from us."
>
> – Hebrews 11:33-40

Hold on, I need a minute. Reading that was hard and I'm choked up. Before I can continue, I need to take a few deep breaths, sip on my coffee and walk around for a minute here in my backyard, where I am writing. Give me a moment to go cry for all of these, for the present day martyrs, the beheaded children of Christians in Iraq, and for the conviction of my own selfishness...

I'm back now, but I must admit that I feel way too small to write this chapter. My life is scarred like every other leader in the kingdom, but as I was walking and crying, I found myself saying, "At least my children are with me." Like many of you, I have endured betrayal, verbal attacks, stalking, anonymous letters filled with lies sent out by cowards, and countless mental battles with unseen forces of darkness. I have walked the floors all night, just like you. I have lived with a pit of despair in my belly, red eyes from countless tears, while holding on to my last ounce of faith. Does that make me weak? No! It makes me a kingdom warrior, just like you. Don't forget the teachings of the Beatitudes in Matthew 5:11-12. Jesus said, ***Blessed are you when they revile and persecute you, and say all kinds of evil against you falsely for My sake. Rejoice and be exceedingly glad, for great is your reward in heaven...***

THE LIST

Here is a list of a few more GREAT MEN who would not be viewed as successes in today's Americanized version of the prosperity gospel. They never pastored mega churches with multiple campuses or had thousands of followers on social media. Yet, they are the founding fathers of the church. Take a moment and read this list slowly:

- Peter – crucified
- Andrew – crucified
- Matthew – the sword
- John – (boiled in oil)
- James, son of Alpheus – crucified
- Phillip – crucified
- Simon – crucified
- Thaddeus – clubbed to death
- Thomas – spear thrust
- Bartholomew – filleted alive & beheaded
- James, son of Zebedee – the sword
- James, brother of Jesus – stoned

- John the Baptist – beheaded
- Paul – beheaded
- Timothy – dragged by horses
- Stephen – stoned
- First Century Christians – martyrs

How did God stand by and watch these tragedies? It's because He already knows the end of the story from the beginning. We are merely seeing a terrible moment in time, but God sees the eternal picture – the glory that is still to come. That why He prefaced this chapter in the Bible with these words: *Hebrews 10:30-36,* ***For we know Him who said, "Vengeance is Mine, I will repay," says the Lord. And again, "The LORD will judge His people." It is a fearful thing to fall into the hands of the living God. But recall the former days in which, after you were illuminated, you endured a great struggle with sufferings: partly while you were made a spectacle both by reproaches and tribulations, and partly while you became companions of those who were so treated; for you had compassion on me in my chains, and joyfully accepted the plundering of your goods, knowing that you have a better and an enduring possession for yourselves in heaven. Therefore do not cast away your confidence, which has great reward. For you have need of endurance, so that after you have done the will of God, you may receive the promise…***

Things that will Make You Cry

Tears are a normal part of the Kingdom warfare; therefore, God does not hesitate to mention many things that will make you cry. But in every case, He also reminds us that there is a special reward in heaven for those. Here is another list of things that will make you cry and the promise that goes with it. This would be a good one to copy and hang where you can see it.

Here is your list:

1. Being hated and excluded

"Blessed are you when men hate you, And when they exclude you, And revile you, and cast out your name as evil, For the Son of Man's sake. Rejoice in that day and leap for joy! For indeed your reward is great in heaven, For in like manner their fathers did to the prophets."

– Luke 6:22-23

2. Suffering and tribulation

"Blessed be the God and Father of our Lord Jesus Christ, the Father of mercies and God of all comfort, who comforts us in all our tribulation, that we may be able to comfort those who are in any trouble, with the comfort with which we ourselves are comforted by God. For as the sufferings of Christ abound in us, so our consolation also abounds through Christ. Now if we are afflicted, it is for your consolation and salvation, which is effective for enduring the same sufferings which we also suffer. Or if we are comforted, it is for your consolation and salvation. And our hope for you is steadfast, because we know that as you are partakers of the sufferings, so also you will partake of the consolation."

– 2nd Corinthians 1:3-7

3. Sickness and disease

"Therefore we do not lose heart. Even though our outward man is perishing, yet the inward man is being renewed day by day. For our light affliction, which is but for a moment, is working for us a far more exceeding and eternal weight of glory, while we do not look at the things which are seen, but at the things which are not seen. For the things which are seen are temporary, but the things which are not seen are eternal."

– 2nd Corinthians 4:16-18

4. Persecuted and struck down

"But we have this treasure in earthen vessels, that the excellence of the power may be of God and not of us. We are hard-pressed on every side, yet not crushed; we are perplexed, but not in despair; persecuted, but not forsaken; struck down, but not destroyed—always carrying about in the body the dying of the Lord Jesus, that the life of Jesus also may be manifested in our body. For we who live are always delivered to death for Jesus' sake, that the life of Jesus also may be manifested in our mortal flesh. So then death is working in us, but life in you."

– 2ND CORINTHIANS 4:7-12

5. Run out of your home or town

"Peter, an apostle of Jesus Christ, <u>To the pilgrims of the Dispersion</u> in Pontus, Galatia, Cappadocia, Asia, and Bithynia, elect according to the foreknowledge of God the Father, in sanctification of the Spirit, for obedience and sprinkling of the blood of Jesus Christ: Grace to you and peace be multiplied. Blessed be the God and Father of our Lord Jesus Christ, who according to His abundant mercy has begotten us again to a living hope through the resurrection of Jesus Christ from the dead, to an inheritance incorruptible and undefiled and that does not fade away, reserved in heaven for you."

– 1ST PETER 1:1-4

6. Grief, wrongful treatment

"For this is commendable, if because of conscience toward God one endures grief, suffering wrongfully. For what credit is it if, when you are beaten for your faults, you take it patiently? But when you do good and suffer, if you take it patiently, this is commendable before God. For to this you were called, because Christ also suffered for us, leaving us an example, that you should follow His steps."

– 1ST PETER 2:19-21

7. Reproach and shunned

"Beloved, do not think it strange concerning the fiery trial which is to try you, as though some strange thing happened to you; 13 but rejoice to the extent that you partake of Christ's sufferings, that when His glory is revealed, you may also be glad with exceeding joy. 14 If you are reproached for the name of Christ, blessed are you, for the Spirit of glory and of God rests upon you.[a] On their part He is blasphemed, but on your part He is glorified. ¹⁵ But let none of you suffer as a murderer, a thief, an evildoer, or as a busybody in other people's matters. ¹⁶ Yet if anyone suffers as a Christian, let him not be ashamed, but let him glorify God in this matter."

— 1st Peter 4:12-16

8. Loss of property

"But what things were gain to me, these I have counted loss for Christ. Yet indeed I also count all things loss for the excellence of the knowledge of Christ Jesus my Lord, for whom I have suffered the loss of all things, and count them as rubbish, that I may gain Christ and be found in Him, not having my own righteousness, which is from the law, but that which is through faith in Christ, the righteousness which is from God by faith."

— Philippians 3:7-9

9. Martyrdom

"When they heard these things they were cut to the heart, and they gnashed at him with their teeth. ⁵But he, being full of the Holy Spirit, gazed into heaven and saw the glory of God, and Jesus standing at the right hand of God, and said, 'Look! I see the heavens opened and the Son of Man standing at the right hand of God!'"

"Then they cried out with a loud voice, stopped their ears, and ran at him with one accord; and they cast him out of the city and stoned him. And the witnesses laid down their clothes at the feet of a young man named Saul. And they stoned Stephen as he was calling on God and saying, "Lord Jesus, receive my spirit." Then he knelt down and cried out with a loud voice, "Lord, do not charge them with this sin." And when he had said this, he fell asleep."

— Acts 7:54-60 Note: Jesus stood up!

10. Anything that makes you cry

"And God will wipe away every tear from their eyes; there shall be no more death, nor sorrow, nor crying. There shall be no more pain, for the former things have passed away."

– REVELATION 21:4

A ROOM FULL OF BOTTLES

I was reading a book many years ago by Rebecca Springer called, "Within Heaven's Gates," and she described a room filled with bottles of tears as she toured heaven in her deathbed vision. So what is the bottle for? That's a question that can only be answered when we get to heaven, but for now I'd like to speculate about what I know and what *could* be...

When Mary approached Jesus with the alabaster box, she broke the box and it filled the room with an aroma. The men in the room chided her for this action, but in her defense, Jesus said that the names of the people in the room would not be remembered, but the story of Mary and the alabaster box would be told until the end of time. And here we are, telling it again. Each of the gospel writers recorded this story and each gave different details. Doctor Luke, who is known for giving details, is the only one who records that she anointed His head with the oil, but washed His feet with her tears and wiped them with her hair. It is interesting that Jesus' last act of blessing for His disciples was to wash their feet. It wasn't because their feet were dirty, but rather He was blessing them.

Many years ago, I took a group of ministers into the deep interior of the Honduras and Nicaragua. Our team traveled by plane, by foot and by canoe to get into the remote parts of the jungle. Several pastors had walked for days to meet us there, many walking barefoot for two weeks in the jungle. They wanted us to share communion with them and in their culture, you never have communion without foot-washing, too. I knelt to wash the feet of those humble pastors who served God in the jungles without pay, without notoriety and most of them, without shoes. The stench in the room, at first, was almost too much, but as I held those twisted, scarred and calloused feet in my hands, I wept uncontrollably. I thought I was blessing them, but as their hot tears dripped on my head while I knelt before them, I realized, I was the one being blessed.

I Can Only Imagine

Just like Mary, one day we may get our moment. Her one moment in time became an eternal legacy. Here goes my imagination again.

"Bryan, you've been summoned by Gabriel to dine with the King today. That's right; Jesus has requested dinner with you in the royal hall. You are allowed to bring one gift if you want to." said the messenger.

"What can I bring the King?" I asked. The messenger smiled and said, "How about your bottle?"

"My bottle?"

"Yes, the bottle with your tears in the great room of bottles."

"How do I get it?"

"Just go to the counter and give them your new name and the name you had on earth." So, I go to the desk in the bottle room. The room sparkles with color, since each bottle is uniquely different.

"May I have my bottle, please?" I ask.

"Yes, what is your name?"

"On earth I was called Bryan Cutshall, but my new name is _____."

"Oh yes, here it is."

"It's not very big. Are you sure this one is mine? I thought it would be larger than that. As matter of fact, I thought it would be in barrels."

"It's not the size of the bottle. Remember this is heaven. Don't you remember the story of the cruse of oil that paid the widow's debt?"

"Yes, I remember, she kept pouring until all the empty vessels were filled," I replied.

"This bottle works the same way. You will pour it on the King's feet until His heart is thoroughly blessed. Then you will seal it up until the next time He summons you."

"How long will this bottle last?" I asked.

The angel replied, "Until every tear is used, every single tear you cried on the earth."

No one but the King knows how many tears are in each bottle.

A Possible Future Event

I walk in the door and a banquet has been prepared for the King and me. Servants line the walls and He asks them to turn around and face the walls with their backs to us.

"I understand you chose to bring your bottle to this dinner," He said.

"Yes, Sir, I did, but I'm not sure what to do."

The King smiles and says, "Just open the lid and pour it on My feet, as much as you want."

I pop the cork of the tiny bottle and begin to pour out a few drops of my earthly tears. As I pour them out, I see the memories of what caused the tears, but I feel no pain in the memories. I only see the purpose behind the memories, and understand why they were necessary for my growth and development.

All of a sudden, something incredible happens! I feel a hot drop on the top of my head. I look up and the King has a bottle in His hand, too. He pours one drop on my head. Tears have been wiped away in heaven, so all of the tears are in bottles. He says, "This is one of the tears I cried with you when you were crying. I knew this day would come and I could rejoice, but I had to watch you cry as you clung to your faith and grew into a strong spiritual man."

Then the King leaned His head back and soaked my tears into His spirit. It was as if it became a part of Him. It was like He inhaled a huge breath the whole time I poured and when the breath came out, it was the greatest laughter I had ever heard. He belly-laughed so hard and so loud that the angels with their faces to the wall were laughing, too. They had seen all of this before. Then I began to laugh. It seemed like we laughed for hours until my spirit was so elated, I could hardly stand. Just before we ate and had the greatest conversation I asked, "What just happened here?" He replied, "The fulfillment of promises just happened." The musicians in the room began to play. The saxophone took the lead and with the most gentle and tender voice, He recited the following verses of scripture:

"Looking unto Jesus, the author and finisher of our faith, <u>who for the joy that was set before Him endured the cross</u>, despising the shame, and has sat down at the right hand of the throne of God."

– Hebrews 12:2

"To console those who mourn in Zion, To give them beauty for ashes, <u>The oil of joy for mourning</u>, The garment of praise for the spirit of heaviness; That they may be called trees of righteousness, The planting of the Lord, that He may be glorified."

– Isaiah 61:3

"Then shall the virgin rejoice in the dance, And the young men and the old, together; <u>For I will turn their mourning to joy</u>, Will comfort them, And make them rejoice rather than sorrow."

– Jeremiah 31:13

"Most assuredly, I say to you that you will weep and lament, but the world will rejoice; and <u>you will be sorrowful, but your sorrow will be turned into joy</u>."

– John 16:20

"For His anger is but for a moment, His favor is for life; <u>Weeping may endure for a night, But joy comes in the morning</u>."

– Psalm 30:5

CHAPTER 10

Paradise

*And Jesus said to him, "Assuredly, I say to you,
today you will be with Me in Paradise."*

– LUKE 23:43

THE GREEK WORD for paradise used in this passage of Scripture is *"paradeisos"* which means *"Eden"*. Let's not stop there; the word *eden* is an Old Testament word found in Genesis and is the name of the garden where God placed Adam and Eve. The word *eden* in Hebrew is *"eden,"* which means *"pleasure"*. So paradise is a place of pleasure.

According to Genesis, Eden is a garden filled with fruit trees, rivers, every exotic animal and flower; a place of unimaginable beauty. It's the kind of place you want to go for vacation. Cascading waterfalls, mountain peaks, seashores, sunrises, morning mists, every fruit known to man. It was a place of innocence and freedom.

WHERE IS EDEN?

Eden was the original paradise. In Luke, Jesus tells the thief on the cross that on that very day, they will be in paradise, together. Eden still exists, but just not on this earth. The next question is—If it isn't on this earth, where is it? The Apostle Paul reveals its new location in 2nd Corinthians 12:1-4.

It is doubtless not profitable for me to boast. I will come to visions and revelations of the Lord: I know a man in Christ who fourteen years ago—whether in the body I do not know, or whether out of the body I do not know, God knows—such a one was <u>caught up to the third heaven.</u> And I know such a man—whether in the body or out of the body I do not know, God knows—how <u>he was caught up into Paradise and heard inexpressible words</u>, which it is not lawful for a man to utter.

Paul states that a language is spoken in paradise that cannot be interpreted in the vocabulary of earth. His exact phrase is *"inexpressible words."* Have you ever had a feeling that you couldn't describe? You wanted to articulate it, but there were just no words that adequately expressed it. That must be how Paul felt. Perhaps paradise is a place that we must "feel" in order to understand it. After all, the word does mean *"pleasure"*.

What Do You Do for Pleasure?

So how do you like to feel pleasure? Is it eating, swimming, soaring on a jetski, or on the back of a quarter horse. Is it lying in a hammock, or by the beach on a blanket or hiking a mountain trail? Maybe it's strolling through paths of beautiful flowers or walking the shores of a beach. Do you like hiking, scuba diving, cooking, reading, watching movies, sports, singing, mountain climbing, or flying? I'm describing HEAVEN. That's right – heaven! Watching movies? I think so – the most incredible adventure stories of how they got to heaven, documentaries of overcoming, the most beautiful love stories! Heaven is not just a place of worship and sacred ceremonies; it's also a place of pleasure. It's paradise.

My Heavenly Itinerary

One of the things I am looking forward to in heaven, is not living on a hectic schedule of meetings, deadlines, travel, emails, and phone calls to return, etc. I'm tired just thinking about all of that - let me catch my breath. Okay, I'm good now; let's continue. I don't know about you, but when I go on vacation, I anticipate the fun things I have planned to do. So, just for our amusement, let's plan a typical day in heaven. Since there is no night there, we can make this day as long as we want. It can even last for years, if we wish. I have had days that were so much fun, I didn't want them to end, so I am sure every day in heaven will be a day like that.

My typical day:

- Worship at the celestial throne room because the seraphim choir has a new worship chorus.
- Adoration time in the presence of the King of kings at the Great White Throne room.
- Meeting John the Baptist for coffee at He-Brews coffee shop.
- Off to Holy Grounds Café for brunch with Elisha the Prophet, Pastor Timothy and my friend, Mitchell Tolle.
- Meeting Faith (my wife) and the kids at the beach for a swim. I am going to challenge Jeff (my son-in-law) to a swim meet now that I have my glorified body.
- Brittany and Lindsay (my daughters) and Sammy and Rosemary (my parents) are bringing lunch from the Loaves and Fishes, one of my favorite restaurants.
- A walk with Macy and Brooklyn (my granddaughters) on the bottom of the sea. I promised we would talk to the fish today since we talked with the elephants and Tyrannosaurus yesterday.
- Going flying with Gabriel and Raphael in the afternoon. I am having trouble with the approach during my landing. My left wing keeps getting tangled on my foot. It's a good thing the celestial atmosphere doesn't allow anyone to crash. There are no broken wings in heaven.
- After flying, I'm meeting Faith (my wife on earth and now my eternal love) to go to a jam session with our

- music friends. Andre Crouch, William McDowell and the Sons of Asaph are doing a jam session together.

- Having a family meeting afterwards to plan our trip to the Constellation of Hercules next week. There are a couple of galaxies we haven't seen yet, so we have to decide which route to take, since there are thousands of ways to get there.

- Going to the lecture hall to hear Billy Graham and King Nebuchadnezzar give their personal testimonies.

- Going fire-walking with Shadrach and Meshech; we are hoping Josephus, Polycarp and Simon Cyrene can join us. I'm also thinking about inviting my friends Hal Santos and Mark Williams.

- Afterwards, I'm taking Macy and Brooklyn to meet St. Nicholas of Myra, you know the "real"…well. He's agreed to wear his old red and white bishop's robe, just for special effects. Of course, with their glorified minds, there is no fooling them anymore. And besides, the old robe has living fibers in this atmosphere, so the suit moves constantly when he wears it.

All of this is just in the first few minutes of the day, since in heaven a day is as a thousand years and a thousand years is as a day.

Can you imagine going to the zoo in paradise? For starters, the animals can talk to you! They have a voice there. Read it for yourself.

> "And every creature which is in heaven and on the earth and under the earth and such as are in the sea, and all that are in them, I heard saying: "Blessing and honor and glory and power be to Him who sits on the throne, And to the Lamb, forever and ever!" Then the four living creatures said, "Amen!" And the twenty-four elders fell down and worshiped Him who lives forever and ever."
>
> – REVELATION 5:13-14

Paradise

Secondly, EVERY animal that has ever existed is there. That includes the dinosaurs, too. Can you imagine talking to a T-Rex or a Raptor? Or how about the deer whose head hung in your den or the fish you ate for dinner? Ok, let's be honest. We could spend years just in the zoo in heaven, especially since there are no cages and we are actually visiting with these majestic creatures of God's creation. I wonder what Balaam's donkey and Jonah's whale will have to say about their side of the story. I can't wait to hear it.

Care to Go Flying on a Horse?

> "And the armies in heaven, clothed in fine linen, white and clean, followed Him on white horses."
> – Revelation 19:14

This story is about the second coming of Christ. He returns from heaven to earth on a white horse and the armies of heaven follow him on flying white horses. Giddy up! Can you imagine soaring through the sky on a flying horse? The thought sounds a little scary, but remember, you are in your gloried body and gravity is no longer an issue. And these majestic flying horses were seen many times in the Scriptures. The servant of Elisha saw them on the hillsides. The prophets saw the chariot and horses separate the prophets Elijah and Elisha, so Elijah could be taken up in a whirlwind. Anyone care to take a ride on a tornado? Elijah did! David heard the sound of these horses in the tops of the mulberry trees in 2nd Samuel 5.

Transportation – "Beam Me Up, Scotty." [4]

How will we get around in paradise? God used many modes of transportation in the Bible. The first mention of mobility was walking in the garden, so walking will still be useful. But there are so many more ways to travel. Jacob saw a ladder that was used by angels. We already mentioned the fiery chariot of Elijah and the whirlwind that took him up to heaven. When Philip, the evangelist, was ministering, he was transported to another city instantly. Jesus walked through walls after the resurrection into a room with locked doors where the disciples were hiding. We've mentioned the flying horses of Revelation 19, but let's not forget the miraculous whale submarine of Jonah or the cherub rides mentioned in Psalm 18. Many believe that we are fashioned like an angel, so does that mean we will get our own set of wings? I don't know. The Bible never mentions wings on Jesus and we are created in His image and likeness (Genesis 1:26), but I do believe we will be able to fly. Jesus was able to take many forms in the Bible; we call those Christophanies. Angels also took many different forms in the Bible. Sometimes they took on the appearance of men and at other times, they were mentioned as standing in the middle of the sea with a rainbow over their heads. So, what if we, too, can take our heavenly bodies and take on other forms? Nothing is impossible in paradise. In our spirit form, we could ride the wind or if we can take the form of another creature, maybe we could run with the elephants. Far-fetched? Perhaps, but remember *"Eyes have not seen, ears have not heard"* and we can't begin to imagine what the Father has in store for us.

Food in Paradise?

I can't imagine what is on the heavenly menus, but we do know the Bible mentions food and eating at the Marriage Supper of the Lamb once we're there. The Tree of Life alone bears twelve kinds of fruit.

Think about all the feasts God required Israel to keep. All of them required ceremonial foods. I can only imagine the feasts in heaven. Banquet tables longer than a football field filled with tables of exotic dishes prepared by angels who were created for the kitchen. There is no diabetes there, so the dessert tables will be incredible. Mile-high meringues and cookie towers standing next to cakes and pies representing every era of mankind, every region of the world, and recipes that are out of this world! Somebody help me! Hmmmm-mmmmm good! If heaven has ice cream and peanut butter, I know I am going to test out my heavenly taste buds and my glorified body. I think all of the great delicacies of this earth will be there. God made them for our pleasure as well as for our sustenance. Paradise is a place of pleasures.

I know there are some people who are going to read this chapter and say we need to crucify the flesh and forget about indulgences of the flesh, but Jesus is the One who asked who needs to fast when you have the bridegroom with you. The struggle of the flesh will be over and we will know the joys of the pleasures the Heavenly Father created for us; and all of it calorie-free. Did I mention it was calorie-free?

Hang on, I need to do the happy dance…Okay, I'm back now.

CHAPTER 11

Peeking through Windows

As we walk through this journey of heaven together, I thought it would be good to interview a few people who actually got to visit there. I know we have the ones in the Bible, but the phenomenon still happens today, and occasionally you meet a person who got to peek through one of heaven's windows. Here are the stories of Alice and Mark, both who are alive and well at the time of this writing.

ALICE OTTINGER, Greeneville, Tennessee

August 22, 1963. Alice Ottinger of Greeneville, Tennessee, was in the middle of childbirth, when her baby died. She was then sedated by the doctors because the baby still had to be delivered. According to Alice, she found herself rowing a boat on a calm, beautiful stream. She described the grass as growing all the way down to the water's edge. She saw beautiful trees lining the river, but there was no underbrush growing beneath the trees. She was rowing toward three people wearing white robes who stood on the stream's edge. Behind Alice, in the boat, was her newborn baby, wrapped in a beautiful blanket. She got to the three people in white robes and then picked up her baby. After holding the baby for a while, she held out her arms to give the people her baby. One of them asked her if she would like to go with them. Alice thought she stepped out of the boat and went with them, but instead found herself waking up in the operating room. She was disappointed when she realized she had not gone with them.

Alice was lying awake in the room when the funeral director came to get the baby, and she watched her husband follow the funeral director out of the room. Still fully awake, Alice watched what seemed to be a giant projector screen appear on the wall. On the screen, Alice saw her Aunt Nana who had died fourteen months before. Aunt Nana was holding a newborn baby and Alice knew that it was her baby. Her aunt had never had children of her own, but had helped to raise everyone else's.

Aunt Nana and the baby were in a field surrounded by butterflies. There was lots of light and no shadows, and everywhere she looked was blooming shrubbery and lots of flowers. It was absolutely beautiful. Alice describes it as more love than she has ever witnessed in her life. The vision faded slowly and Alice laid her head back on the bed, completely at peace that her baby was with the Lord and was being lovingly cared for by Aunt Nana. A great peace settled in Alice's heart and mind that day after the heavenly visitation and vision, and it has lasted to this day.

MARK SKAGGS, St. Louis, MO

Mark Skaggs lives in St. Louis, Missouri. He had hip replacement surgery on September 9, 2013. During his physical therapy, two days later he collapsed due to a blood clot that traveled from his hip, through his lungs, and passed through the right ventricle of his heart. Mark was without oxygen for approximately 33 minutes. During that time, they kept trying to resuscitate him. After 13 minutes, they were going to pronounce him dead, but a nurse noticed his eyes blink. She continued to work on Mark to try to save his life. Again, another 13 minutes passed without much success. They were ready to pronounce his time of death again; when the same nurse who so diligently refused to give up on him, heard a slight poof of air come from his mouth. She again began to resuscitate him and this time was successful. By the hand & grace of God, Mark was alive. During this 33-minute resuscitation process, 11 of his ribs were broken. The doctors didn't know the extent of his brain damage due to the fact he was without oxygen for such a long time. Along with his heart stopping, so did his kidneys. Mark does not remember any of this; instead he remembers another story:

Mark remembers walking in a meadow. He describes the colors as unlike anything he had ever seen and too vivid for vocabulary. He felt a gentle breeze blowing on his face and was walking toward the most beautiful lake he had ever seen. As he got closer, he noticed a man in a long purple robe sitting on the ground just looking at the lake. It was not just any kind of robe. He remembers it being two to three inches thick. It was the most plush garment he had ever seen. Mark described the robe as being trimmed in gold and having a hood on it. The robe was so elaborate that—even now—he stumbles each time he tries to put it into words! He walked over and sat by the man in the purple robe.

Mark describes an atmosphere of total peace. He sensed no fear or pain at all. Mark's hands were on his knees as he sat on the ground. He never saw the person's face, but all at once, the man in the robe reached out his hand and laid it over Mark's hand there on his leg. The man never spoke a word. Mark describes a feeling coming over him of warmth and love, and to this day, begins to cry each time he gets to that part of the story. Together they stared at the lake which was so large he could see no shore line in any direction. Soon the man got up and walked away and Mark looked and saw another person walking toward him. This was a man he knew, DJ Haynes, who had passed away a few months earlier. DJ was wearing a white robe and walked over to Mark, and placed his hand on Mark's shoulder. That is the moment Mark began to recover and rejoin the land of the living, waking up back at St. Anthony's hospital. Mark was sitting in church a few weeks later on Palm Sunday, when a man can on the stage dressed as a Roman soldier and told how witnessing the crucifixion changed him. He described the scene where they put a purple robe on Jesus. That was the first moment that Mark knew for certain, the man in the purple robe was Jesus and one touch from His hand changed Mark's life forever.

PAM BREWER, The Carolinas

Pam Brewer writes, "Often the Lord speaks to me through dreams. This dream was different though." Here's her story: I remember my senses being sharper than I would have even thought were possible. I don't remember the way I traveled to heaven, I just was there. The first thing I noticed were people I knew had died coming to greet me. They were so happy to see me. I was taken from one person to the next and greeted with such love and joy I had never known before. I knew that God was there even though I never saw Him; I could sense His presence so very deeply and lovingly. No matter where I went, He was there. I noticed the streets were a deep rich transparent gold. I had read the Bible through many times before but Revelations 21:21 always drew me to the pearly gates and not the streets. The fact the scriptures spoke of the transparent gold streets had not caught my attention in all those years.

Next, I noticed was the river that was flowing was so rich in color and so very clear. There were trees in the river but the river did not have banks. The water seemed to be alive and knew where it needed to travel. I saw beautiful houses. There were brilliant colors throughout heaven that even reflected on the water, and danced off the houses. One time my husband asked me to explain the colors. I was not able to find the words because we don't have anything that compares. The closest I have ever heard to describing the colors was in a sermon which Bryan Cutshall preached about heaven. He said the colors were like looking through a kaleidoscope. Somehow I knew the colors were reflecting from God Himself.

Everything seemed so alive and there was a joy that is unexplainable. Even the joy seemed to be a living presence. It was a dream that I shall never forget. As I reflect upon the dream, it stirs a presence inside me which faintly resembles what I felt in the dream. It causes me think that we are not yet capable in these earthen bodies to know and experience that deep presence as we could not contain His glory.

At a women's conference several years ago, I told some ladies at a table about this dream. Across the room a lady stood up and asked if she could finish telling my dream. Even though I thought it was strange, I agreed. She picked up on the part where I was telling about the river. I had not yet gotten to the part about there not being any banks. It wasn't long until I realized we had been given the same dream. In a flash of a moment we both even sensed that deep love, joy and peace in each other. I could tell she was experiencing it as she had walked over beside me. She told me that she saw and sensed the same in me. All of these things together have given me an even stronger desire to truly be one with others in Him. I have found in doing so is the only way to experience anything like the joy, love and peace that was felt in this wonderful glimpse into heaven.

Deacon Stephen the Martyr – One More Peek Through Heaven's Window

> "When they heard these things they were cut to the heart, and they gnashed at him with their teeth. But he, being full of the Holy Spirit, gazed into heaven and saw the glory of God, and Jesus standing at the right hand of God, and said, "Look! I see the heavens opened and the Son of Man standing at the right hand of God!" Then they cried out with a loud voice, stopped their ears, and ran at him with one accord; and they cast him out of the city and stoned him. And the witnesses laid down their clothes at the feet of a young man named Saul. And they stoned Stephen as he was calling on God and saying, "Lord Jesus, receive my spirit." Then he knelt down and cried out with a loud voice, "Lord, do not charge them with this sin." And when he had said this, he fell asleep."
>
> — Acts 7:54-60

These open windows are mere glimpses of the wonders and splendor of heaven.

> *Heaven's sounding sweeter all the time,*
> *Seems like lately, it's always on my mind.*
> *Someday, I'll leave this world behind.*
> *Heaven's sounding sweeter all the time.*
>
> — Jimmy Swaggart[5]

CHAPTER 12

The Kings of Heaven

*Grace to you and peace from Him who is
and who was and who is to come,
and from the seven Spirits who are before
His throne, and from Jesus Christ,
the faithful witness, the firstborn from the dead,
and the ruler over the kings of the earth.
To Him who loved us and washed us
from our sins in His own blood,
<u>and has made us kings and priests
to His God and Father,</u>
to Him be glory and dominion forever and ever.*

– REVELATION 1:4-6

ON THE EARTH, kings are given power, authority and wealth to govern the earth. They are set over people to lead them with a visionary heart. They have provision.

It is my belief that God raises up certain kings on this earth to bring provision for the vision.

THE STORY OF ONE OF HEAVEN'S QUEENS

"Then, six days before the Passover, Jesus came to Bethany, where Lazarus was who had been dead, whom He had raised from the dead. There they made Him a supper; and Martha served, but Lazarus was one of those who sat at the table with Him. Then

Heaven on My Mind

> Mary took a pound of very costly oil of spikenard, anointed the feet of Jesus, and wiped His feet with her hair. And the house was filled with the fragrance of the oil. But one of His disciples, Judas Iscariot, Simon's son, who would betray Him, said, "Why was this fragrant oil not sold for three hundred denarii and given to the poor?" This he said, not that he cared for the poor, but because he was a thief, and had the money box; and he used to take what was put in it. But Jesus said, "Let her alone; she has kept this for the day of My burial. For the poor you have with you always, but Me you do not have always."
>
> —John 12:1-8

Two Questions:

I want to start off with two questions from this story in the Bible:

1. Why did it bother Judas so much that Mary offered an elaborate gift?

2. Why did Mary give such an extravagant gift?

There are two hearts displayed in this passage. One is the heart of selfishness and the other is a heart of generosity. This story takes place two months after Lazarus had been raised from the dead.

First, I want us to answer question one. Why did it bother Judas so much that Mary offered an elaborate gift? The answer is Judas was selfish. Selfishness and being self-centered is the enemy of generosity. Judas made it sound like he cared for the poor, but that was only a ploy to get his hands on the money. Judas had the offering box and he would take money out of the offering box from Jesus' traveling ministry. I'm sure we can't think of doing such a thing, but the truth is, when we refuse to tithe and give offerings, it's the same thing. Keeping what belongs to the Lord is the same as stealing what belongs to the Lord. It is the refusal to recognize that God gave us everything we have. Our small tithe back to Him is merely a test of our faith that God is our resource.

The second heart displayed in this story is the heart of generosity. Generosity can take you to new levels of blessings in your life. Mary gave an entire year's wage as a gift. A denarius is equivalent to one day's wage, subtract her one day off a week, the Sabbath, and you will see that she gave an entire year's wage. The point of this story in the Bible isn't about the amount of her gift, but the extravagance of her generosity. Think about it for a moment, no amount of money can impress God. Gold is pavement in heaven and jewels are stones in the walls. How much money would it take to impress God? God doesn't see the amount; He sees the heart of generosity. Mary was generous because her brother had been raised from the dead. When a member of your family dies or you or a loved one has been spared from death, it completely changes your view about material things and worldly possessions.

Levels of Giving in the Bible

There are 3 levels of giving in the Bible: Tithes, Offerings and Extravagant Offerings. You can trace every gift to one of these levels.

When tithes are given, the windows of heaven are opened up and we receive blessings that we can't contain. That is the promise of Malachi chapter 3. God also told us that He would rebuke the devourer for our sake and also restore the years of loss. Tithing opens up heaven's blessings to us on this earth.

There are many extravagant offerings in the Bible:

1. Solomon offered thousands of sacrifices.

2. In today's market prices, David gave over $145 BILLION to the building of the temple, just in gold and silver.[6] That doesn't count bronze, wood, craftsmen…

3. The widow gave two mites. It takes 4 mites to equal 1 penny. And Jesus said she gave more than anyone because she gave all she had.

Truly, the heart of generosity.

The Eternal Rewards of Generosity

Mary's story is told in the Bible three times: Matthew 26, Mark 14 and John 12.

> "Assuredly, I say to you, wherever this gospel is preached in the whole world, what this woman has done will also be told as a memorial to her."
>
> – Mark 14:9

Because God is a rewarder, Mary is going to receive a blessing *every time* this story is preached throughout the whole world. Consider the ripple effect of her blessing for one act of elaborate generosity. Now, add the compound interest to her investment in heaven. Do the math: one year's wages with interest in heaven every time someone has preached or told this story for the past 2000 years! WOW! What Mary will receive in her heavenly bank account is so much more than she gave! She didn't give to get back. She gave expecting nothing in return. It was her way of saying "thank you" to God, but Jesus blessed the moment with an eternal blessing.

There is a pastor in Zimbabwe today winning his community and Mary is getting rewarded for it in heaven because of her generous act.

Steve and Melody Dulin, of Dallas, Texas, teach business seminars called *How to Operate Your Business God's Way*. They have given away 50% of their business income each year to the work of the Lord for over 20 years. A few years ago, he was looking at his accounts and adding up what he had. He looked at his checking account. He checked his business account. He tallied his investment account, and then his retirement account. The next morning during Steve's quiet time, the Lord asked him, "Steve, how much money do you have?" He knew the answer because he had just looked it up. He replied with a question, "Well, what do you mean?" The Lord inquired a second time, "How much money do you have?" then asked, "Will you give it to me?"

Steve said his first thought was fear. Then he thought, "God, I know You don't ask this of very many people. You must have a reason." and he decided to seek God and act on his faith. Steve and Melody agreed that God was asking for it, and they did it. They gave it all away. One year later, the Lord said to Steve, "How much money do you have?" Steve hesitated to answer because he knew what had happened a year earlier. He went and added it all up and all four accounts were twice what they were a year ago. God said, "See? In one year, I've done twice what it took you almost 20 years to do." Steve said that had never happened before nor since, but it taught him to listen to God. **God is a rewarder.**

Heaven's Kings

The eternal kingdom of heaven is a kingdom of kings and priests. Both have authority and eternal honor. Both wear specific garments and I believe attend gatherings prepared only for kings or priests. I have spent some time talking about priests in this book, but now I want to focus on the eternal kings of heaven.
Let's look at Revelation once again.

> "Grace to you and peace from Him who is and who was and who is to come, and from the seven Spirits who are before His throne, and from Jesus Christ, the faithful witness, the firstborn from the dead, and the ruler over the kings of the earth."
>
> "To Him who loved us and washed us from our sins in His own blood, and has made us kings and priests to His God and Father, to Him be glory and dominion forever and ever."
>
> – Revelation 1:4-6

Who is in this heavenly royal family of kings? As I said before, on the earth, kings are given power, authority and wealth to govern the earth. They are set over people to lead them with a visionary heart. They have provision. It is my belief that God raises up certain kings and these individuals are given wealth on this earth to bring provision to the vision or God's appointed visionaries. If they understand their calling and use their wealth for this purpose, I believe they will be the kings in heaven. Their test of kingship will be on this earth, but their reward of kingship will be eternal honor in heaven.

Revelation, chapter 5, is a Throne Room scene. It is one of the most descriptive ceremonial pictures in the entire Bible. Reading it is almost like watching a movie. It takes you step-by-step through a ceremony and describes various crowds of people who are present. We get to hear the choir sing, we see the Elders falling down to worship, we hear the voices of angels, and even have a heavenly guide taking us through the ceremony, like an emcee. Two of the groups present in this heavenly scene are kings and priests. They are seated together in the ceremony. They have a heavenly status that others do not have. Yes, everyone gets to go to heaven, but our glory and honor will not be the same there. We will walk in the glory of how we served our King of kings in the faithfulness of His calling.

I believe the kings of heaven will be those whom God raised up on this earth to bring provision for the vision. Some gave millions, others gave mites but all gave generously and that is what the record of heaven will show.

CHAPTER 13

Body Language

*If I have told you earthly things and you do not believe,
how will you believe if I tell you heavenly things?*
— JOHN 3:12

THE BIBLE TELLS us in 1st Corinthians 15:50 that flesh and blood cannot inherit the kingdom of God. Let's read the next three verses:

> "Behold, I tell you a mystery: We shall not all sleep but we shall all be changed in a moment, in the twinkling of an eye, at the last trumpet. For the trumpet will sound, and the dead will be raised incorruptible, and we shall be changed. For this corruptible must put on incorruption, and this mortal must put on immortality."

<u>*We shall be changed*</u> is very exciting language, but changed into what? The rest of the verse says that we who are mortal will become immortal and our corruptible bodies will become bodies that no longer decay, age, get injured, fight disease, or get sick. Exciting so far? Read on, because it just gets better. What will that body look like? Will we all get to be heavenly super models or built like pro athletes? The Bible doesn't mention anything about curves and muscle tone, but it says quite a bit about the difference in a terrestrial body, which is the one we have now and a celestial body which is the one we will have in heaven.

1st Corinthians 15:40-44 reads, *There are also <u>celestial bodies and terrestrial bodies; but the glory of the celestial is one, and the glory of the terrestrial is another.</u> There is one glory of the sun, another glory of the moon, and another glory of the stars; for one star differs from another star in glory. So also is the resurrection of the dead. The body is sown in corruption, it is raised in incorruption. It is sown in dishonor, it is raised in glory. It is sown in weakness, it is raised in power. It is sown a natural body, it is raised a spiritual body. There is a natural body, and there is a spiritual body.*

Are you still with me? We die in one body and we wake up in another one, that's all it means. We die in a natural body that deteriorates every second and we wake up in a new body that cannot be corrupted, be dishonored or even get weak. I know the question that is on everyone's mind, are we going to be angels? Or maybe some of you were thinking, do we still have all of our body parts, and if so, what is the function of them in heaven? Both are great questions and the Bible gives us the answer to both.

Are we angels in heaven? Before we answer this question, we need to understand that there are many different types and classifications of angels in heaven, each with their own uniqueness, purpose and glory. There are cherubim, seraphim and archangels which all look different and have totally different assignments. Cherubim are the guardians of heaven. You can read about them in Genesis 3:24, Exodus 25:18-20, Ezekiel 1:4-28 and Ezekiel 10:1-22. Lucifer was cherubim. Okay, so get the Valentine's day card out of your mind or the Renaissance paintings showing baby angels with diapers or carrying bows, arrows and harps - Uh, not a cherubim, not even close! Cherubim are mighty and are large and in charge; literally, they are in charge. The Bible calls Lucifer a cherub that covers. If you read that in Hebrew, it is literally saying, that he was over other angels. 'Covers' means that he was a covering for other angels or another way of saying it would be that he was their leader or boss.

Seraphim are also mentioned in the Bible. They are always depicted as worshipping. The sing, they speak, they fly, they encourage one another, and they glorify God through worship. One of the most vivid portraits of seraphim in the Bible is found in Isaiah 6. Listen to the language of this scripture:

> "In the year that King Uzziah died, I saw the Lord sitting on a throne, high and lifted up, and the train of His robe filled the temple. Above it stood seraphim; each one had six wings: with two he covered his face, with two he covered his feet, and with two he flew. And one cried to another and said: "Holy, holy, holy is the Lord of hosts; The whole earth is full of His glory!" And the posts of the door were shaken by the voice of him who cried out, and the house was filled with smoke."

Did you get cold chills as you read it? I know I did. These are huge six-winged angels that cry out, **"Holy, Holy, Holy is the Lord of hosts"** as they fly around God's throne room. We have no reason to believe these are the only ones, for all we know there could be millions of them. In Ezekiel, it says they have four faces: a man, an eagle, a calf, and a lion. Okay, maybe you don't want to *look* like seraphim in eternity, but you may want to make friends with one. They are majestic and powerful.

The Bible also talks about archangels; you remember, don't you? Michael and Gabriel? Daniel 10 gives a vivid portrait of them both; one in battle and the other one on a mission.

Gabriel is the one who shows up in the Christmas story. As a matter of fact, every time we see him in the Bible, he is on a mission to bring someone a word of instruction and encouragement from God. Michael, on the other hand, is always the protector and defender. The Bible calls him "the defender of Israel." At least two times in the Bible, Michael stands up to Satan. In the book of Jude, he disputes with him over the body of Moses and in Revelation 12, he kicks Satan out of heaven. I like this guy!

The only thing we know about the appearance of archangels is that every time someone sees them, they have to say, "Don't be afraid, I'm on your side." It could be their mere size or perhaps their glowing skin. Maybe it's the fact that we don't see people with wings on a daily basis and that one fact along could be quite startling. Anyway, they are not afraid of a fight, even a big one.

So, do you still want to be an angel? How about the four faces of the seraphim or the might of the cherubim? Want to war like an archangel or do you have something else in mind for eternity? Actually, you and I will look more like Jesus when He appeared to His disciples after the resurrection. They didn't recognize Him at first because He had been glorified, but once they got used to the changes, they knew it was Him. He even showed them His scars. I really don't think you have to keep the scar from your appendectomy in heaven, I think Jesus kept His scars because He is the ultimate sacrifice for man. His scars are part of His glory. They are beautiful scars of love. The Bible says in Philippians 3:20-21, *"For our citizenship is in heaven, from which we also eagerly wait for the Savior, the Lord Jesus Christ, who will transform our lowly body that it may be conformed to His glorious body..."*

1st Corinthians 15:49 reads, *"And as we have borne the image of the man of dust, we shall also bear the image of the heavenly Man."* We will be a new breed of citizen in heaven. We will be the first of our kind, those made in the image of God, redeemed by God and glorified by God. We will sing a new song that the angels cannot sing, "I'm redeemed." Hallelujah!

A glorified body that looks like Christ still has all the body parts. As a matter of fact, the Bible says the first thing we are going to do in heaven is eat. That's right! There is a banquet prepared called the Marriage Supper of the Lamb. Remember at the last supper Jesus said, **I will not drink this cup again until we come into the fullness of the kingdom.** After Jesus rose from the dead, He ate breakfast on the side of the Sea of Galilee with His disciples. He walked down the road to Emmaus and had a long conversation with two men in Luke 24. As a matter of fact, He spent the night with them and ate a meal with them. It wasn't until He broke the bread that it was revealed to them that they were eating with Jesus. He walked, talked, ate, and even slept. Does this mean we can do all of these things in heaven? Heaven is going to be a real life, not a moment of worship suspended for all of eternity. It will be a real life of walking, talking, eating, and living.

What about all my body parts? I knew you were going to ask that, so here's all I know. Now you know you get to keep your eyes, ears, mouth, and legs. How about everything else? Will there be males and females in heaven or are angels genderless? It doesn't matter if angels are genderless, we will not be angels. Angels cannot sing the song of the redeemed. We will be a new breed of citizen in heaven. Keep in mind that God designed food and sex, as well as all the natural appetites of man. The argument of many is from Luke 22:34-36, which reads, *Jesus answered and said to them, "The sons of this age marry and are given in marriage. But those who are counted worthy to attain that age, and the resurrection from the dead, neither marry nor are given in marriage; nor can they die anymore, for they are equal to the angels and are sons of God, being sons of the resurrection.* The question Jesus is answering is about a person who gets remarried after their spouse passes away. They were asking, "Which one will she be legally married to in heaven?" This is not referring to sex; it is referring to legal marriages. Jesus merely says that in heaven we don't get married or give our daughters away in marriage anymore. Honestly, He never said anything more on the subject other than that. Okay then, we will be *like* angels. Angels ate with Abraham, they slept with the daughters of men in the Genesis, they rode horses and chariots, they worship, and do thousands of other things. The point is, heaven is a real world with a real life! You are going to *live* there, not *exist* there. I can't answer the sex question with Scripture, but I will leave you with this thought; if sex is only for procreation, we will certainly have no need for it in heaven. On the other hand…well, you will just have to ask the rest of your questions on the subject when we get there.

One of the things I am most looking forward to in heaven is talking to angels about the other side of the story. You know, where the car didn't hit the tree or where the check showed up in the mail at just the right time, or the one where the fever broke or the disease disappeared. I can just hear them now, "Well, what happened was…"

CHAPTER 14

To Infinity and Beyond[7]

I CAN ONLY IMAGINE that one day these words will come out of my mouth: *I'm in heaven! Oh my word, I'm really here! Really, really, really here! Can you believe it? We are actually here. Somebody pinch me. Oh, heaven, heaven, heaven, heaven, heaven! We are actually here. In heaven! The.Real.Heaven. (sigh) (deep breath) Do you see that? And that? And that? Is that...? I think it is! I thought he would be taller. Do you hear that? Do you smell that fragrance, what is it? I've got to get me some of that. Can you believe how far we can see? How far we can jump and oh my, we can ....fly? YES! (happy dance) I always wanted to fly; now I can. But where do I fly first, there is so much to see, so many people I want to talk to. Oh yes, and Jesus, I want to see Him first. Can you believe that music? How many octaves is that? How many instruments is that? Can you believe the size of that choir? Oh my! Who do I talk to first? Where do I go first? What do I eat first? There is so much color here, and so much light. Rainbows, waterfalls, mountains and more. It's all here. Is that a giraffe? Oh my! It IS a giraffe and he's talking to a lion. Did I say talking? I really meant to say... They really ARE talking! Hey, would you look at that? I can't even pinch an inch. ♫♪ Hallelujah! ♫♪ Hallelujah! ♫♪ Hallelujah, Hallelujah ♫♪ Halle-lu-jah! Happy dance, happy dance—I'm doing the happy dance. I'm skinny – finally. What? Everybody's skinny. Well, I'll be.....! But somehow, it doesn't seem to matter anymore. I'm actually in heaven! I'm strong; I have no worries, no pains, no enemies, no bills, wow...no bills! No problems to solve, no employees to calm down, no schedules, no deadlines, no flights to catch, I'm really here—I'm in heaven. Honey, is that you? And I didn't think you could be more beautiful, but here…wow! Kids? Wow, you look good with halos. Dad, Mom, Grandma, Grandpa, you are so young, so healthy, so happy! They're all here—family, friends, and people I've worshipped with, the lady at the grocery store, all of them, all of those who gave their life to Jesus and served God. There is so much to do, so much to see, so much to learn, so many mysteries that are about to be revealed. Hey angel, can I touch your wings and maybe your halo, too? What is that? Seraphim! Wow! Who knew they were so big? Can they see and talk out of all four faces on their head? So much to learn, so many questions, so much adventure ahead. Hey Moses, is that really you? Whew…at last! I'm here. I'm actually in…you know…heaven!*

Alright, now you know I'm going to go a little bonkers when I get there. Maybe you have plans to just sing a song and play a harp, but not me. I plan to get my "dance on." I want to see it all, experience it all. And I probably will say all of those things and a whole lot more. I read about the 30 minutes of silence in heaven, I'll try, but, I've got a lot of questions and a lot of people to see. *Elijah, were you scared riding on that tornado? John, did it hurt when they cut your head off? Ok, stupid question, of course, it hurt. Daniel, what did you do in the lion's den - were you sitting or hugging the wall? Did you sleep or pray or cry in the corner or wet your pants? I know I would have certainly done the last two in a den of lions.* So many questions for so many people! Heaven!

Okay, it sounds like heaven has everything and it does. But there is so much more to the story. Heaven is not just a city; it is a new reality of everything, literally.

When I was a kid, we used to sing a great old hymn titled, <u>When We All Get to Heaven</u>.[8] I loved that song and still do. It says, *"When we all get to heaven, what a day of rejoicing that will be! When we all see Jesus, we will sing and shout the victory."* As a kid, I use to think that heaven was the eternal Sunday morning worship service. I thought we would all hop from cloud to cloud and play harps with baby angels in diapers with bows and arrows, kind of like the ones on a Valentine's card. Did I mention that's when I was a kid?

I have since learned that heaven is more than a city. God literally recreates everything.

Here it is in Revelation 21:1-5:

> Now I saw a <u>new heaven</u> and a <u>new earth</u>, for <u>the first heaven and the first earth had passed away</u>. Also there was no more sea. Then I, John, saw the holy city, <u>New Jerusalem, coming down out of heaven from God</u>, prepared as a bride adorned for her husband. And I heard a loud voice from heaven saying, "Behold, the tabernacle of God is with men, and He will dwell with them, and they shall be His people. God Himself will be with them and be their God. And God will wipe away every tear from their eyes; there shall be no more death, nor sorrow, nor crying. There shall be no more pain, <u>for the former things have passed away</u>." Then He who sat on the throne said, <u>"Behold, I make all things new."</u>

Why do you think God is going to make a new heaven and a new earth? I think it's because we will live there, visit there and explore there. Where? Everywhere—the heavens and the earth! I've had the privilege of traveling to almost all the continents and many countries, but there is so much I've never seen. Yet, God made it all for His glory. In eternity, I can see it all. I can visit Hawaii, the Swiss Alps, the jungles of Africa, the rivers of Asia. And in our glorified bodies, we can walk on the bottom of the sea, walk into volcanoes and hike Mt. Everest without gear. The earth is the Lord's and it's been created to bring Him glory and honor. The universe is so vast that the earth is like a mere speck of dust just in our own galaxy. And still there are hundreds of millions of other galaxies in the universe and many that no eye of technology has ever seen. It just sits there day in and day out singing the praises of the Creator of the Universe. Galaxies are still being born all the time and universe expands itself into infinity and beyond each day. One day, God will give us the time to go see it all.

> "But, beloved, do not forget this one thing, that with the Lord one day is as a thousand years, and a thousand years as one day."
> – 2ND PETER 3:8

Indulge me for a moment. If a day is 1,000 earth years, what if we get to explore the world for six days and then come "home" for a day of worship, just like now? What if we get to go on a 6,000 year adventure and come back for a 1,000 year worship service in heaven? And that is just the first week. The process repeats itself throughout all of eternity. I can just see it now, my wife and I are jogging on the rings of Saturn, *(we don't jog together now, but remember, we have glorified bodies then—happy dance again)*. We are on the rings of Saturn and we hear the shofars blow, calling all of God's children back to New Jerusalem for the Sabbath, the day of worship.

As we approach the celestial city, we hear the choir of angels welcoming us home. There, we praise and worship, hear testimonies of "how we made it" with God's help. Then, perhaps part of our praise is to tell what we just experienced during the week while we were away. The whole place erupts in praise as we talk of God's wonders and His creative genius. We may even say to ourselves, "That place sounds amazing, let's go there next." What if that is life in heaven? What if heaven is really to infinity and beyond and then back home again for worship? Back to the Father's house for unimaginable, unfathomable, indescribable worship! Worship that fills the soul, energizes us, invigorates us, and cleanses us. And just when you think it can't get any better, the week starts all over again…while the ages roll on. I can only imagine!

CHAPTER 15

Many Rooms

My Father's house has many rooms; if that were not so, would I have told you that I am going there to prepare a place for you? And if I go and prepare a place for you, I will come back and take you to be with me that you also may be where I am.

– John 14:2-3 NIV

The King James version of the Bible translates verse two in this wording, *"in my Father's house are many mansions."* Some say, "If I get a mansion, it's a house all to myself." Others say, "I'd rather have a bedroom at the Father's house." Both ideas are missing the point, since there is no night in heaven, I doubt if we will need a bedroom at all. I think the point is that there is a "place for us", whether that is a bedroom, a mansion, a palace, or a city, there is a place for me. However, the term "many rooms" implies so much more than bedrooms. Don't forget that John saw the city of God, New Jerusalem, coming down from heaven and it was a city 1400 miles square with twelve levels in it. What are on those twelve levels; mansions, neighborhoods, buildings, or restaurants? And that is just the city of New Jerusalem. We will have the galaxies to explore. If God takes the time to make a new heaven and a new earth, I don't think the earth will just be one gigantic garden. Will there be buildings on the earth, or on the other planets? Let's look deeper into the possibilities of "many rooms."

I think a great place to start is with what we already know exists in heaven. How about a quick overview of just the rooms John saw and recorded in the book of Revelation. Let's see, there is the throne room that he mentions many times, starting in chapter four. John also saw a library, a banquet hall, a choir room, a room where prayers are poured out as incense, and there must have been a stable for the many horses he saw. He saw a city of pure gold, which is transparent. Gold in its purest and most refined state is clear like glass. So, the city of gold would look like a city of glass to us.

We know there is a temple there, because the tabernacle of Moses and the Temple of Solomon were replicas of the heavenly temple. Since food is mentioned many times, I am guessing there are restaurants and banquet halls that are filled with the many flavors, textures and spices God created for us to enjoy. Food was not just given for sustenance; it was also one of God's many pleasures to enjoy. The trees of life in heaven bear twelve different kinds of food and the bread of heaven also has to be baked, so you can just imagine the smell in the streets of fresh-baked bread and pies cooling in the window sills. There is bread on the table of shewbread in the temple. I sure hope bread served at the marriage supper includes yeast rolls. Since sin will be removed, maybe we won't have to eat unleavened bread all the time. Yes, I vote for yeast rolls.

One of the things we will do in heaven is tell our stories to one another. I can't wait to hear the inside story on the Red Sea parting or Noah's Ark. I'm pretty sure Mrs. Noah has a different story than the simple line "and it rained forty days and forty nights." She lived on a floating zoo; it has to be quite a story from her point of view.

In her classic book, *Within Heaven's Gates*, Rebecca Springer describes heaven from a vision she had on her deathbed. She was brought back from death to write the book and tell her experience. She mentions a place she visited called the Great Hall. It is an open air, massive structure made of jasper columns and amethyst floors. I can just see the glistening green columns overshadowing the purple amethyst floors. On one occasion, she mentions going to hear a lecture by Martin Luther and John Wesley, when suddenly from behind a curtain, the King appeared and explained heaven's view of the same incidents the two men had just described. We only see one side of reality now, but there is also heaven's view. I can't wait to hear my guardian angel tell me about some of the rescues he did for me; things I didn't even know about!

Since John saw a city filled with jewels, there might be places like jewelry stores, especially since in heaven many people are bedecked in jewels. There might be shoe stores because there is no mention of people going barefoot in heaven. Since there are crowns perhaps other hats are worn, as well. Don't forget we are mixing the styles of many eras. Just because the saints are robed in a white robe at the Resurrection Ceremony in Revelation chapter 7, doesn't mean we wear it forever. It could just be ceremonial attire. Just because robes are mentioned, we don't have to assume that we wear the same garment for eons of years. Maybe some of the "rooms" are for your wardrobe. Can you imagine a walk-in closet in heaven? I'm sure HGTV would love to air that one—too bad. Perhaps you and I will choose our garments for the occasion, so maybe there is shopping. Now, I bet you're glad you laid up treasures in heaven. Now you have spending money.

Let's not stop with the rooms in a city, because John also saw a new heaven and new earth with restored beauty to the state of the Garden of Eden. There will be gardens, perhaps even mountain chalets or resorts. I am sure the earth is not restored to a wilderness state, so we may go to the new cities that are built and visit magnificent structures. Heaven is a real life so there must be concert halls to enjoy music. I can't wait to hear some of my favorite artists perform with their glorified voices. Wow! I just got goose bumps, thinking about it.

There is no mention that we lose our talents when we are glorified, so I choose to believe all of the gifts that we used to glorify God in this life will continue to glorify Him throughout all eternity. "But, Bryan, I can't sing, what am I going to do?" you may ask. Just do what you do: cook, write, sew, garden, give lectures, build something, grow something, make something, love others, serve, or drive a high speed car. I'm just sayin'. We don't have to go back in time to go to heaven. Perhaps every era of time is there and we can visit any time we choose to visit. Maybe we go to the first century this week and visit the days of Moses next week. Remember eyes have not seen, ears have not heard, neither has it entered into the heart of man, the things God has prepared for them that love Him. Besides, that wouldn't be the first time someone traveled forward or backwards in time. Philip was translated to another city. Moses saw the entire Promised Land from Mt. Nebo in a heavenly vision and also saw the entire creation story and the rest of the book of Genesis on Mt. Sinai. That's how we got the book of Genesis. Daniel saw the future which he called the end of days. That's our time now. Can you imagine Daniel trying to describe airplanes and computers from his day? No wonder he was sick for days after his vision of the future! John saw the city of Jerusalem at the time of the second coming, and he was on the Isle of Patmos and Jerusalem had already been destroyed by the Romans. So, time travel is nothing for the Almighty. Maybe you can do more than remember the Alamo; you might be able to visit it. Sorry AAA, no trip tix for these adventures.

If heaven is a real place with a real life, I am sure we will use our gifts and talents there to serve the Kingdom. Who knows? We may even have jobs. Not the kind with inter-office conflicts, long hours and politics. No, perhaps we do something we love doing, something we enjoy and so get the fulfillment of blessing others with our God-given gifts. If that is true, then the rooms of heaven could contain everything from museums, art shows, concert halls, food courts, clothing stores, and much more.

What if heaven has neighborhoods? Ok, indulge me for a moment. I know I'm stretching you. What if we get to live near all the people we love? What if we get to live in the house with our families and live next door to our friends? Maybe we go to the temple together for worship or to the art district for concerts and lectures. Maybe we go on picnics down by the river of life or by a lake or a snowcapped mountain. Maybe we stroll a beach or hike a rain forest trail.

At the beginning of time, God designed a world for us to live in; He called it Earth. Notice the Bible doesn't say, in the beginning God created the heavens and Mars, Jupiter, Neptune, Pluto, Mercury, and so on. It only says, ***In the beginning God created the heavens and the earth.*** The earth was God's special place that He carefully crafted and designed with the atmosphere, elements and resources to sustain life. In doing so, God also designed beauty and pleasure as a part of that world. He wanted us to love our home.

I can only imagine what beauty and pleasure God has designed for us in eternity. My mind can only compare it to the things we have here on earth that bring us joy, but I am quite certain that even with a good imagination, we are not even scratching the surface of His design. When my kids were away in college, Faith and I would start preparing for them to come home for Christmas. She would decorate the house with Christmas trees and lights to create a wow factor when they walked in the door. I would put lights on the outside of the house so when they arrived they would have this feeling of being welcomed home and that someone had been anticipating their arrival. We would stand on the front porch waiting for them. The sight of the lights and their parents waiting for them would cause them to break out into the biggest smiles as they pulled into the drive way. Can you imagine the preparation that has gone into God's ultimate family reunion? The Heavenly Father has been anticipating all of His children being home for thousands of earth years. I am sure the angels are getting things ready. If I close my eyes and think on heavenly things, I can almost see the lights of that city! Smile!

CHAPTER 16

Well Done

When I first started writing this book I used the title "Well Done Factor" as a working title. Sometimes I do that to keep my focus and then later come up with a different title that I think may say more to the person who is wondering what the book is about. For me, this book is about the "Well Done Factor." You may be asking yourself, "What in the world is that?" My point exactly, and that's why I didn't make it the title of the book. However, here's my moment to describe what I think may be the highest point of my existence, both in heaven and in my time here on the earth.

I have always believed that we were made for a purpose; not just from the collision of sperm and egg and random gene mixtures. I know that part of us looks like our parents and we do take on family characteristics in other ways, but I have always believed that we existed before that moment. This may be a stretch of the imagination and perhaps theological concrete, but it's a belief I have deep down in my gut. I believe we exist in heaven before the collision of sperm and egg. That may be the moment of conception, but at what point in that instant does the embryo receive a living eternal spirit? At what point do we declare that unborn composition a living being? When is it "alive"? When is it a person? I am very pro-life because I believe unborn babies are also born spirits. Freaked out? Then, try these Scriptures on for size and see if you can explain them without believing that every unborn baby is already a born spirit.

> "For You formed my inward parts;
> You covered me in my mother's womb.
> I will praise You, for I am fearfully and wonderfully made;
> Marvelous are Your works,
> And that my soul knows very well.
> My frame was not hidden from You,
> When I was made in secret,
> And skillfully wrought in the lowest parts of the earth.
> Your eyes saw my substance, being yet unformed.
> And in Your book they all were written,
> The days fashioned for me,
> When as yet there were none of them.
> How precious also are Your thoughts to me, O God!
> How great is the sum of them."
>
> — Psalms 139:13-17

> "Listen, O coastlands, to Me,
> And take heed, you peoples from afar!
> The Lord has called Me from the womb;
> From the matrix of My mother He has made mention of My name."
>
> — Isaiah 49:1

Here's one more, just for fun.

> "Before I formed you in the womb I knew you;
> Before you were born I sanctified you;
> I ordained you a prophet to the nations."
>
> — Jeremiah 1:5

Thinking about it yet? Okay, just hold my hand and I'll walk you through the rest. We are sons of God because the Spirit of God dwells in us. You good with that? But we are also a spirit! We are a body, soul and spirit. Where did our spirit come from? I believe it came from God. I believe we once existed as a part of Him. I cover this in another chapter, but let me give you this illustration again to make my point.

Once I had a dream/vision (not sure which one), and in it, I saw God reach inside of Himself and pull out what appeared to my eyes as a ball of light. He would take one from His arm, hold it in His hand and press it into a body and the body would come to life. For the next one He might take the light from His head, His feet or His belly. Each time, He would take a part of Himself and press this light into a human body and it would come alive. Is there a Scripture about that you ask? The closest thing I can find is when God breathed into Adam and a figure of clay became a living being. It was a transfer of God's breath into Adam. The word breath is also translated "spirit." God is a spirit. And we are spirit and flesh.

Therefore, if we are born of God and our spirit is from God, we have God's DNA in us. Not only that, we have purpose. I love Jeremiah 29:11 because it says, ***"I know the plans I have for you, declares the Lord."*** I really believe God has a plan for each of us. We were not all created to do the same things, accomplish the same things or to compete with one another. Everyone seems to want to be someone else, somewhere else and something else. However, we were created to find our true self and to glorify God with the gifts and talents He gave us.

Sometimes, I wonder if He will show me the moment of my spiritual inception. Perhaps He waited for the gene pool to stop scrambling and then based on that elaborate and unique design, said, "I'll give you this part of me." Or maybe it's the other way around. Maybe my spirit got there first and danced with the genes to form an image that looked like my heavenly Father. Think about this. If God really has distributed "parts" of Himself in all of us, then the best way we can show God to the world is to be the best "us" we can be. Being you is the best way to bring honor and glory to God.

The most epic moment in eternity will be when we stand before the Father and hear two words, "Well done." Exactly what do you think those words will mean?

The context of this Scripture is found only in Luke 19, in the Parable of the Minas.

Here it is:

> "And he said to him, 'Well done, good servant; because you were faithful in a very little, have authority over ten cities.'"
>
> – Luke 19:17

We also hear the Father say, *"This is my beloved son in whom I am well pleased."* He did this at the baptism and when Jesus transformed into His spirit likeness on the mountain with Peter, James and John. You remember — Elijah and Moses showed up and Peter wanted to build a church there.

However, "well done" is only mentioned in this one parable. The parable is about business and investment. Let me summarize the story for you. A master gives ten men the same amount of money and instructs them to go invest it. He returns to inspect the investment. Each of them had done different things with his money. One did nothing, but decided to bury it. To the one who used it wisely, he said, "Well done, you have been faithful over a few things, so now I will make you the ruler over many things." He gave them authority and rewards based on their stewardship of his gift to them. For me, this will be the high point of my existence. If I hear Him say, "Well done," that means I used the part of Himself that He invested in me and used my God-part, my God-nature to bring honor and glory to the Creator of the Universe.

I don't know when this will happen — maybe at our coronation when we receive our crowns, or the day we arrive and receive our new name and garments. It could be a sit-down dinner with Him. Who knows? I'm not sure.

"Well done" could mean, you did business well. It could mean, you sang well, you taught well, you wrote well.

It could mean you danced well, played well, ran well, designed well, cooked well, created well, painted well, coached well, tutored well, traveled well, built well, swam well, piloted well, judged well, doctored well, discovered well, worked well, talked well, typed well, carpentered well, soldiered well, parented well, cleaned well, fished well, boated well, flew well, dreamed well, counseled well…

There is no end to this list, just like there is no end to His nature. Just be the best you and you will represent the best Him.

CHAPTER 17

Children in Heaven

I REMEMBER BEING TAUGHT a prayer as a boy, and praying it every night before I went to sleep. Maybe you remember this children's prayer, too.

Now I lay me down to sleep.
I pray the Lord my soul to keep.
If I should die before I wake,
I pray the Lord, my soul to take.

Okay, honestly, I never knew as a child I was praying to go to heaven, if I died in my sleep. Only years later would the words of this prayer hit me hard when I was asked to speak at the funeral of a baby who was full term and died during the birthing process. For the first time in my life, I began to ask the question, "If I should die before I wake, what happens to me then?" From that time until now, I have had a firm belief that when children or babies go to heaven, they simply grow up there. I don't believe they die an infant and instantly become an adult in heaven with no past, gifts, talents, testimony or purpose. I think they have their own story, their own teachers, their own classrooms, and their own purpose.

Isaiah 54 is an unusual chapter in the Bible. It starts out by dedicating the chapter to the childless woman. Verse 1 reads, *"Sing, O barren, You who have not borne! Break forth into singing, and cry aloud, You who have not labored with child! For more are the children of the desolate, Than the children of the married woman," says the Lord."* The next verse tells her to add a room to her house or in this case, her tent. By verse eleven, it addresses her pain. *"O you afflicted one, tossed with tempest, and not comforted, behold, I will lay your stones with colorful gems, and lay your foundations with sapphires."* It basically says that the foundation of her life has crumbled, but in the rubble God has placed treasures, literally jewels. In verse 13, He gives the barren woman an unusual promise. Remember she has no children in her house, but God says to her, *"All your children shall be taught by the Lord, and great shall be the peace of your children."* Wow! Your children will be taught <u>by the Lord</u>. What a revelation!

I believe that every child who does not get to grow up on the earth grows up in heaven. I also believe that every couple who has lost a child or children on the earth has treasure in heaven that others do not have. In the crumbled foundations of their lives, there lies a promise. There is treasure in the rubble! There are jewels in the broken foundation of disappointment and pain.

Let me explain it in a story. This is not a Bible story. It's a story of how I imagine this scene may take place in heaven. Let's say a woman or man dies or is raptured and they get to heaven. As they arrive, they are met by many familiar people so that they feel safe. These people are loved ones they knew on the earth. Let's say they just walked through the tunnel of light that many people who have experienced death and came back have witnessed and reported. On the other side of the tunnel, they walk into a green meadow with a brook and blue skies. It looks as though they have arrived at a picnic. The people waiting for them are all people they have known and loved on earth. They are people they haven't seen since they passed away and the reunion is filled with joy, laughter, strong hugs, and stories. It may only last for minutes but in heaven's time, it may feel like days, for no word, phrase, expression, or detail is ever lost. All is savored! After the short welcome home reception, one of them says, "I know you want to see the Master, He's expecting you." They walk with you into the celestial city and take you to the Palace gates. You are met there by someone you know very well; someone you have never personally seen, but one who is ever so familiar. It's your guardian angel. You know instantly when they call you by name. And without explanation, you just know they were with you for your entire life. They held you, carried you and even pushed you at times. This familiar guide takes you on the Palace tour and to the place where the Master is waiting for you. "He's just beyond this door," your guardian says. "Don't be nervous, it will be just like all of the other hundreds of talks you've had with Him, just as comfortable and just as intimate."

You walk beyond the door to a private room where He waits for you. There is no one in the room but you and the Master. After an extended visit, He says, "I have someone I want you to meet and I want to go with you." It is your son or daughter. To some He may say, "Let's go see the rest of your children." He walks with you to your new home, a house with many rooms; a house with your personality. Each member of your family has their own room for private visits from friends, family, patriarchs, celestial citizens, and the Master. As you arrive to your new home, you see them waiting on the front porch. They run to you and call you "mother" or "father" or perhaps a name that your children on earth called you. They say, "We have so many things to catch up on. I want to show you my nursery and those who cared for me as a baby. I want you to meet my teachers and see my school. I want you to meet all my friends that I have grown up with here in the neighborhood. I want you to meet the one I love, who loves me." It may seem like months go by as you walk through the rubies, sapphires and diamonds that were hidden in the rubble on the day your foundation crumbled on the earth. Soon you realize that your baby grew up without knowing pain, sorrow, sickness, or rejection. All your child knew was love, joy, friendship, and peace. Soon it will be time for a new family photo when the rest of the family arrives safely home.

CHAPTER 18

Will We Go to Church in Heaven?

I THINK MANY PEOPLE have it in their head that heaven is one loooooooong worship service for eons of years. I disagree with that idea. Heaven is a real life of social activities, responsibilities, pleasures, adventures, celebrations, ceremonies, and yes, it does include worship on levels we can't even imagine. Just think of the redeemed and the angels singing together. Think of a testimony service, when Daniel steps up and gives glory to God for delivering him from the lions' den, followed by Shadrach, Meshach and Abednego. Goose bumps yet? Asaph leads a chorus, with Chris Tomlin and Steven Curtis Chapman singing a duet on one of the verses, then John and Charles Wesley sing the next verse. Kari Jobe, Darlene Zschech and Israel Houghton sing on the praise team along with Miriam, the sister of Moses, King David, and the heralding angel choir. Gabriel and David Thrush do a horn duet and a hundred thousand instruments join in symphony. Martin Luther gives an exhortation followed by Martin Luther King. T.D. Jakes, Joyce Meyer, and Billy Graham, and then Charles Haddon Spurgeon finishes. When they are through, the Apostle Paul preaches from his famous sermon on "this mortality must put on immortality." Okay....I'm on a plane right now, but I need a praise break... (I'm rejoicing as much as is allowed on a red-eye morning flight from Roanoke to Atlanta.)

Heaven Has a Tabernacle

Before I get into this, I need to explain something. Revelation 16 talks about a temple in heaven, but after the final judgment of the earth is pronounced, the temple is no longer needed. Revelation 22 says in the city of New Jerusalem there is no temple there. Why? Well, a temple is a place where you go to seek God. A tabernacle is a place where someone dwells. Heaven no longer needs a temple because it now a heavenly tabernacle. God is with us! God dwells with us and we dwell with Him. No longer are prayers offered as petitions and no longer do we need to fast to seek His presence. His presence is EVERYWHERE. We dwell in Him and in the atmosphere of heaven, His presence is always felt.

> "And let them make Me a sanctuary, that I may dwell among them. According to all that I show you, that is, the pattern of the tabernacle and the pattern of all its furnishings, just so you shall make it."
>
> – Exodus 25:8-9

> "And see to it that you make them according to the pattern which was shown you on the mountain."
>
> – Exodus 25:40

> "Now this is the main point of the things we are saying: We have such a High Priest, who is seated at the right hand of the throne of the Majesty in the heavens, <u>a Minister of the sanctuary and of the true tabernacle which the Lord erected, and not man.</u>"
>
> – Hebrews 8:1-2

The Tabernacle has three sections: the outer court, the inner court and the Holy of Holies. There are five pieces of furniture that lead you to the door of the Holy of Holies. It starts with the Brazen Altar, which represents our salvation. Next is the laver, which is our sanctification. From there, you move from bronze furniture to gold furniture, and you move into the inner court of the priests. In the inner court, there is a candlestick which represents the work of the Holy Spirit through men, the table of bread representing the Word of God, our

Bible, and finally the altar of incense which represents prayer. All of this leads you to the throne of mercy called the Mercy Seat.

THE MERCY SEAT

The Ark of the Covenant is a coffin.[9] Yes, you read that right; it was a coffin. You know — a casket. There is no dead person inside of this coffin, but there are four things that represent man's rejection of God. The coffin contains the Ten Commandments on the original stone tablets, the rod of Aaron that budded, a golden pot filled with manna, and the first Torah scroll written by Moses. The coffin was overlaid with gold and had two Cherubim facing each other on the lid. When placed in the Holy of Holies, the Ark of the Covenant represented the throne of God on the earth and that is why it is called the Mercy Seat. God would manifest His presence in a cloud showing that He was occupying His throne. It wasn't a pretty white fluffy cloud. It was a storm cloud with lightning and thunder in it. The Ark was the manifestation of God's physical presence on earth (the Shekinah). When God spoke with Moses in the Tent of Meeting in the desert, He did so from between the two cherubs. After the ark was moved into the Holy of Holies in the Tabernacle, and later into the Temple, it was accessible only once a year, and then, only by the High Priest, who would approach the mercy seat to ask forgiveness over the sins of the people.

When the High Priest entered the most holy place, he would sprinkle blood on the Ark of the Covenant, the coffin. It was necessary for the blood to cover the things that were inside of it. God gave us the 10 commandments, but we rejected it. God gave them a High Priest, represented by the rod of Aaron, but we rejected it, too. The golden pot of manna represented God's miracles and yet which Israel said their souls loathed. God gave us the Torah, the Bible, but we rejected it, too. None of these things were able to reconcile us back to God. They all revealed our sins but could not remove them. However, the blood of a perfect man, Jesus, on the mercy seat removed our judgment leaving only the alternative — His mercy for us. Up to this point, it sounds like a great Old Testament story, but there's more.

> "But Christ came as High Priest of the good things to come, with the greater and more perfect tabernacle not made with hands, that is, not of this creation. Not with the blood of goats and calves, but with His own blood He entered the Most Holy Place once for all, having obtained eternal redemption."
>
> – Hebrews 9:11-12

During the three days Jesus was in the grave, He went to heaven and offered His own blood in the heavenly tabernacle. He poured His blood on the mercy seat of heaven. To prove this had been done and that our mercy was complete, He gave us a view of it on resurrection morning, the day we call Easter.

> "But Mary stood outside by the tomb weeping, and as she wept she stooped down and looked into the tomb. And she saw two angels in white sitting, <u>one at the head and the other at the feet,</u> where the body of Jesus had lain."
>
> – John 20:11-12

It is the last portrait of the mercy seat. Two angels at the head and the feet of a coffin, but this time, the tomb is empty. This time, there are no objects of rejection, no objects of judgment inside the coffin. This time, the tomb is empty. Mercy is completed!

So I guess I need to answer the question about whether or not we go to church in heaven. We will not go to a temple and worship; the tabernacle of God is now His presence with us always. In every corner, on every street, in every room, in every meadow, stream and mountain, He is there. There is no need to go to church in heaven, church has come to you. The sound of worship fills the atmosphere. The glory of God lights every path, every doorway and every room. The enlightenment of God renews every mind. His presence brings joy, unspeakable. It brings peace, eternal. It brings life, everlasting. It brings love, unending.

Welcome to the Father's House, you are finally home!

CHAPTER 19

Living Water

I HAVE TO ADMIT that when I think of living water, I think of things living in the water like tadpoles and growing microorganisms. Somehow, I don't think that's what Jesus had in mind when He told the woman at the well that He could give her living water and she would never thirst again. Just think for a moment about the significance of water and God's plan.

First of all, the entire planet was under water in the beginning, and God divided the water from the water in Genesis chapter one. The only geographical landmark given for the Garden of Eden is four rivers that come together in the garden. Then God flooded the whole earth with water again in Noah's day. He designed humans and plants to consist of about sixty-percent water.[10] Water is needed for life to exist – anywhere. Jesus' first miracle was turning water into wine. He walked on water, and He chose to perform the majority of His miracles around rivers or lakes. Do I have your attention yet? Water is obviously significant to God. I understand the need for water on the earth. Rain, dew, snow, and springs allow things to grow. Most of the earth is salt water and that also provides a home for the foundation of our food supply. But, is water really needed in heaven?

There is a river in heaven called the River of Life. What makes it even more interesting is that its source originates from underneath the throne of God. Read this scripture very slowly or you will run right past all of the clues.

> "And he showed me a pure river of water of life, clear as crystal, proceeding from the throne of God and of the Lamb. In the middle of its street, and on either side of the river, was the tree of life, which bore twelve fruits, each tree yielding its fruit every month."
>
> – REVELATION 22:1-2

This river intrigues me because of how it is described. Let's unpack it s-l-o-w-l-y: *a pure – river – of – water of life, – clear – proceeding from the throne*. And it may even have a street in it, but then again, John could have been talking about a street in the city. But you never know; this is heaven. Am I the only one who thinks this is a really big deal? I think it is. It's just as important as the gates of pearl and jasper walls, except this river is not just for beauty. It has a purpose; it is the water of life. Not only is it important, it's so important that one of the last things God says in the entire Bible is come and get a drink from this river. *Revelation 22:17,* ***And the Spirit and the bride say, "Come!" And let him who hears say, "Come!" And let him who thirsts come. Whoever desires, let him take the water of life freely.*** This verse is almost the last verse in the Bible. I say almost because there are only four more verses after it in the Bible. It's an invitation to come to heaven and drink this water of life. Curious, isn't it?

Does this water sustain us? Do we drink it every day, or only one time and then never thirst again? Is it a metaphor or is it real water? I know it's a real river, since the throne is real, the trees are real, and the fruit is real. So yes, the water is real, too, but why is it there? Do the trees of life need it to live, is that why they grow on a riverbank?

In Rebecca Springer's classic book, "Within Heaven's Gates", the book I've mentioned in previous chapters, she describes a scene where she visits a lake and a river. She describes the lake as looking like liquid gold, except it was transparent. She tells about lots of light dancing all through the lake. I know this sounds strange, but she describes the lake as though it had layers, or maybe different floors would be a better way of saying it. She didn't really swim in it, but walked in it, stretched out and floated. She even describes hearing music while she was suspended in the deep waters. The purpose of the lake was to energize people. She talks about walking into the lake with friends and going several hundred feet deep and suspending themselves at that depth. There, they carried on conversations and just floated effortlessly without fear, limitation or restriction. She states that is was like knowing total peace and that when they walked out, they were renewed with fresh energy. The lake in her vision was fed by the River of Life. She describes a river, a lake and a sea.

Okay, by now you are used to my wild imagination so just let me run with this for a moment and see where we end up. Let's see what we've go to work with. So far, we have the fact that God chose water to sustain life on the earth from the beginning. Secondly, the words of Jesus about the living water, and then there is the scene that Ezekiel and John the Revelator saw where the river was flowing from the throne of God. Oh yes, we can't ignore one of the last verses in the Bible, an invitation to come and drink from the river.

Well, let's see, I could go with a fishing trip, a heavenly baptism by John himself or maybe Rebecca Springer's day at the lake. But I think I'll go a different way. Day one, arrival to heaven—you get to drink from the water. Only one drink and you never thirst again. I like it so far, but it's not enough or else it could just flow from a cup like the widow's oil jar in Elijah's day. Okay, John mentions a river and he also mentions the sea of glass. So we have a river and a sea. Day two is filled with more happy reunions, worship, talking animals, angels, and so forth and so on. Now two days in heaven is about two thousand earth years, so you might be ready to move on to other things. (*ref. 2 Peter 3:8*) So day three is going to be – walking on water lessons. Oh yes, I really like this one. Moses is there to part the water so the melancholy types[11] can touch the sides and see the bottom. Jonah sits on the banks and tells a fish story while you wait and Peter shows up to make sure it's done right, since he had more practice than most. Then He, you know who I mean, the One, the true One, the Mighty One, the Holy One, the only One, walks out into the water and says, "Come." The same One who said, "Come and drink," now says, "Come and walk". And there you are with your family cheering you on and you take your first step of faith in walking on the water.

Far-fetched, you say? Peter might have an argument with that. Of course, you know Jesus wasn't just a water-walker. He was a storm-walker and a wave-walker. One lesson at a time; still waters today and waves tomorrow.

Well, by now you know, I haven't had a vision about heaven, I didn't die and come back to tell a story, but I do read the Bible and nothing in this story is new. It's all happened before and it might just happen again with you as one of the characters in the story. Are you ready to dance?

CHAPTER 20

A New Name

Timothy Bryan Cutshall - that's the name my parents gave me. I think they just liked the combination of names, but I was curious about the meaning of the names, so I looked up the etymology of each one.

> **Timothy** – This is a masculine given name. It comes from the Greek name *Timotheos*, meaning "honouring God", "in God's honour", or "honored by God"
>
> **Bryan** – This name is derived from Old Celtic language meaning "high", or "noble". Bryan is the surname of the given name, Brian.
>
> **Cutshall** – The story handed down to me from my ancestors was that the true family surname is the German family name of 'Gottschalk', which means "servant of God." When our ancestors migrated to the U.S., they pronounced their name in their strong German brogue, and the people who wrote down their name at Ellis Island wrote it phonetically the way they pronounced it. Somehow 'Gottschalk' became 'Cutshall' on paper. Because they were in separate lines, my grandfather had brothers who legally spell their name 'Cutshaw' instead of 'Cutshall'. The Cutshaws and the Cutshalls are the same family.

So if you put together the names I inherited, Timothy Bryan Cutshall, it literally means, "a nobleman, honored by God, because he belongs to the family who are servants of God." At the time of my birth, my parents chose names they liked, but is has proven to be prophetic, as my family members are Levites who serve in the House of the Lord, for which He has honored us all.

Known As You Are Known...Hmmmmm?

"For now we see in a mirror, dimly, but then face to face. Now I know in part, but then I shall know just as I also am known." Many people interpret 1st Corinthians 13:12 to mean that in heaven you will be known by the same name as you are called on the earth. I hope not, since on Facebook® there are at least seven other Bryan Cutshalls. If you read the entire passage, you will easily understand that it means we only see things in part on this earth, but from heaven's view, we will see the complete picture of life. Another way of translating this verse would be, in heaven I will be fully known, instead of partially known.

A New Name

> Revelation 2:17, "He who has an ear, let him hear what the Spirit says to the churches. To him who overcomes I will give some of the hidden manna to eat. And I will give him a white stone, and on the stone <u>a new name written which no one knows except him who receives it</u>."

> Revelation 3:12-13, "He who overcomes, I will make him a pillar in the temple of My God, and he shall go out no more. I will write on him the name of My God and the name of the city of My God, the New Jerusalem, which comes down out of heaven from My God. And <u>I will write on him My new name</u>. He who has an ear, let him hear what the Spirit says to the churches."

White stones, new names, pillars in the temple, are you sure we are talking about heaven? Yes, we are talking about heaven. Some of these passages are a little more difficult for us to wrap our head around from our modern world point of view. Most of our churches don't have pillars in them now, and we are not accustomed to giving people white stones.

The meaning of the white stone is a bit mysterious because it is a method that is not commonly used in the Bible. As a matter of fact, this verse in Revelation is the only place in the Bible where this practice appears. But remember, John is the one who wrote the Revelation of Jesus Christ and gave it to us as a sacred book. John most likely understood the giving of the white stone from some of the cultural practices of his day.

A small object called a "tessera," made of stone, clay, bone or even wood, conveyed special privileges to its owner. The ancient Romans used tesserae as tokens of admittance to events in the arena. Perhaps the white stone in Revelation is like a key, which opens a door, or maybe a ticket of admittance into reserved banquets for the victorious ones in heaven.

One very likely explanation could be the ancient Roman practice of awarding white stones to the victors of athletic games. The winner of a contest was awarded a white stone with his name inscribed on it. This served as their ticket to a special awards banquet. Jesus promises the overcomers entrance to the eternal victory gala in heaven. The "new name stone" could easily be an eternal signet, like a super bowl ring, worn by all champions in heaven. Perhaps it gains them entrance to certain ceremonies held only for those who fought hard battles and overcame by faith. This promise is not given to all believers, but rather to all overcomers, or champions.

When God set up the priesthood, he told Moses to make a breastplate for the high priest. This breastplate contained twelve stones, one for each of the tribes of Israel. Each of these stones had the name of one of the twelve tribes of Israel engraved on it according to Exodus 28:21. As he ministered in the temple, the high priest bore the names of God's people into God's presence. In the same manner, the "white stone" with the believer's name written on it could be a reference to our standing in God's presence.

Since I have not hesitated to speculate in this book, I'd like to "only imagine" again what this white stone is like. Let's start with the two names that we are going to be given, "our new name" and "His new name." Let's suppose then that the white stone and the pillar in the temple are related to the same type of honor.

Here We Go...May I Borrow Your Imagination for a Moment?

An announcement is given all through heaven by the heavenly heralds. They fly through the air, like a streak of light, with a scroll in hand, announcing that a special ceremony is being held in the throne room and all are expected to attend. By this time, all of the residents of heaven have arrived and are very settled in. All have been given robes of righteousness, have been assigned to their heavenly mansion and have already begun their endless reunions with family, friends, Bible characters, and saints from every age and race. But on this day, all of the activity ceases and everyone gathers in the throne room. Is it big enough, you ask? Isaiah 66:1 tells us, **"Heaven is my throne and the earth is my footstool."** It's a big as the universe itself, so there is plenty of room. All gather! After a song from a girl who had previously only sang in her church of thirty people while on the earth, the King steps forth to explain the purpose of the gathering.

"We have already gathered, to crown heaven's kings and queens. We have already gathered to crown our martyrs, shepherds, evangelists, and those who were hospitable. Today is not about crowns, it's about champions. There are those among us who endured hardships that caused others to collapse. There are those who kept the faith in the face of losing everything. There are others who lived with broken hearts, yet found enough room for faith and love to be preserved through the brokenness. There are those who walked blind paths of faith, who endured sleepless nights of fear and worry in order to take the gospel to the world. Today, we affirm heaven's champions, the victorious ones, those who have overcome!"

As each person's name is called, they step forth to the platform of champions. There is no bronze, silver or gold, there is only the white stone. Each of given a white stone, which looks almost transparent like a diamond. As each champion steps forward, their story is told by their guardian who transcribed their story in the Book of Life.

The angel gives intimate details that were forgotten by the champion. The angel recounts details such as, "I was there when she fell to her knees and cried out to God, because all seemed lost." Other testimonials ring out, "He prayed anyway. She sang anyway. He trusted God anyway. She gave anyway. He moved anyway. She loved anyway. He forgave anyway." and so on.

The Voice of Many Waters spoke, "You have been known as (Bryan), but now you will be known as (New Name)." And just like Abram became Abraham, Jacob became Israel and Saul became Paul, each champion is given a new name. The white stone is hung from a silver chain placed around the champion's neck. The angel then declares, "This stone will give you entrance to the champions' hall and special events that honor the works of each champion. Come when you are summoned and join the banquet of the kings and champions." In addition, the King adds, "You are given a reserved place in the tabernacle. In there, we have many pillars with many names written on them. Each of the pillars is reserved near the King's throne. You will stand there on the days of worship and worship with the kings and champions in the places of honor that are designated for you."

As the champions are called, each reacts with surprise and humility. You see, on the earth no one knew most of their names. Yet all the while, they were famous in heaven—and in hell—for their great faith.

CHAPTER 21

The Cloud of Witnesses

> "Therefore we also, <u>since we are surrounded by so great a cloud of witnesses,</u> let us lay aside every weight, and the sin which so easily ensnares us, and let us run with endurance the race that is set before us, looking unto Jesus, the author and finisher of our faith, who for the joy that was set before Him endured the cross, despising the shame, and has sat down at the right hand of the throne of God."
>
> – Hebrews 12:1-2

The Witnesses

Imagine you are in a race. You're running out of energy and willpower when all of sudden, you pass a section in the arena where the old champions are sitting. As you run by them, they leap to their feet and cheer for you! As they applaud, you recognize they are the older generations of champions who have already finished the race you are running. Energized by their encouragement and example, you kick it up a notch and keep running.

This is as close as I can get to describing the scene of Hebrews 12. Keep in mind, Hebrews 11 is the Hall of Faith chapter where we have heard the heroic feats of God's champions. Now we are told they are sitting in the grandstands of heaven, cheering us on to finish our race. Finally, the world champion, the universal hero, the King Himself is pictured in the grandstands with them. We are told to look at Him, Jesus. The Son of God became the son of man, so the sons of men could become sons of God. *Fix your eyes on him*, the writer says, and you will be able to finish your race. Look to the joy that is set before you and you can keep going!

Clouds

Why does the writer refer to this group as clouds of witnesses, why not a group of witnesses, or a grandstand of witnesses, or maybe even a choir of witnesses? This particular word in the Greek can literally be defined this way, "a shapeless collection of people, a throng or multitude." Our mind goes to stratus and cirrus clouds, but he is referring to the cloud metaphorically as a shapeless volume of people. Keep in mind that this cloud of witnesses is not comprised of angels. These are people who have lived on the earth, in particular those mentioned in Hebrews 11: Abel, Enoch, Noah, Abraham, Moses, and many others. This cloud of witnesses grows each time a person leaves this earth and goes to heaven. So, add in the names of those you know who are cheering you on. I would have to add the names of pastors, teachers, elders, and intercessors who have impacted my life. It strengthens me to know their encouragement did not stop when their life on earth ended. They are still there – now with a whole cheering section - *You can make it! Keep going! Never give up!*

The Big Test

Just to give you a heads up, I'm leaving the Biblical context for a while and I'm going to my imagination again. You should be used to this by now. Here goes…

Imagine with me — A few people meet up in heaven who haven't seen each other in a while. I'll use the names of some of my best encouragers who are now on the other side. Dave, Rabon, Ralton, Jesse, and Elmer meet up and one of them says, "Did you hear that Bryan is about to take the big test of faith? God is going to ask him to do something that is so out of his comfort zone that it will require the greatest step of faith he's ever taken in his ministry."

The old gang decides to join the cloud for my big race. Along the way they tell Mary, Donna, Carrilea, and Anna about the big test.

Now on the earth, I have no idea what is going on in heaven. I find myself restless and on some days, even hopeless. One of God's highest praises for His saints is that they had faith during "wanderings." So God chooses to test me through wandering, and my encouragers gather to cheer me on.

In reality, wandering feels like you are lost, blind and confused. You find yourself crying out, "Where are You, God? Why aren't You answering me, Lord, and why can't I feel Your presence?" The truth is, He hasn't moved, but in His providence, He has hidden Himself from our spiritual sight. We are like a child lost in a mall.

At first, we just wander around looking and then, reacting in our humanness, we start to panic. Anxiety creeps into our thoughts. Our hearts beat faster, and we start to feel the tightness in our chest. We feel alone, haunted, like we're being stalked, and it's unnerving. However, it's all part of the plan to strengthen our faith and it is necessary to take our trust to the next level. As we wander, we begin to lose hope. We lose sight of our goal and start to shut down emotionally. But just before we quit, we find a note we kept from one of our encouragers who has passed on. Then we find a Scripture marked that they gave us when we needed a word from God. Before long, we have a memory of them praying for us, and the next thing we know, we are surrounded by the comfort of those on the other side.

I think sometimes they may even get special permission to visit us in our dreams. The Apostle Paul said that we only see through one side of a two-way mirror (1st Corinthians 13.) But if we could see the other side of reality, we would see the throng of people cheering us on, pointing out the signs that they left behind for us to find.

Imagine for a moment that you can really see the cloud of witnesses. Who is in that group for you? What are they saying? How are they gesturing to you? Can you feel the strength, the pull of their encouragement? "Keep going," they cry, urging us on. "The best is yet to come!"

The Rest of the Story

Don't stop yet, there's more. Now suppose that one of your blessings in heaven will be to read the diaries of the cloud of witnesses from the day of your big test, or the season of testing. Maybe one of the blessings will be to hear how they influenced you in a season when you felt so alone. You may hear of battles fought between angels and demons while you thought you were just stalemated and waiting. You may hear how God ordered your steps with His Word and allowed them to be a part of rerouting your path on the earth. Who knows how many nights they sat at your bedside, how many days they never left your side or how many songs they sang to your spirit? I know this idea may seem a little off-track for conservative theology, but really it's not that far-fetched at all. The last verse of the Gospel of John reads, *"And there are also many other things that Jesus did, which if they were written one by one, I suppose that even the world itself could not contain the books that would be written. Amen. John 21:25.*

Perhaps the scribes of heaven will allow us to read the behind the scenes chapters of battles and victories. Revelation 20:12 reads, *"And I saw the dead, small and great, standing before God, and books were opened. And another book was opened, which is the Book of Life. And the dead were judged according to their works, by the things which were written in the books."* Notice the phrase, *"and books were opened."* Nothing more is said about these books in the Bible, but since the next book mentioned in that verse records our works on the earth, perhaps the "other books" tell the rest of the story.

CHAPTER 22

Another View of Eternity

A FEW MONTHS BACK, I was on a ministry trip with my good friend, John Brockman. In Texas, we were picked up by a driver whose name was Dave. While on the way to the airport, he overheard us talking and asked if we were ministers. After confirming that we were, a conversation followed that I will never forget. At first, he was just getting to know us, but he overheard me telling John that I had almost finished my new book on heaven and had been writing part of it on our flight from California to Texas. I told him about the chapter of this book titled, *Peeking through Windows* and that I was looking for people who had died, gone to heaven and then lived to tell the story. Dave asked, "Have you talked to anyone who went to hell and lived to tell the story?" I replied that I hadn't met anyone who had that kind of story. For the next several minutes, John and I sat intensely silent as our driver told us the bone-chilling experience he had many years earlier. Soon after the story, we arrived at the airport. John and I laid our hands on Dave, prayed with him, and blessed him.

THE STORY OF DAVID DESJARDINS

In 1982, a 23-year-old man named David Desjardins, called "Disco Dave" by his friends, was at the end of his rope. He was living with his girlfriend and her children in a small trailer in the bayous of Louisiana. During a severe bout with depression, a voice kept telling him to end it all. He stood in front of a mirror to slit his wrist and as the knife came down he fell backwards and hit his head on a bath tub. It was at that moment that he felt himself lifting above his body and could see his lifeless, bloody corpse on the floor. In Dave's own words, he said, "The body above was sucked back into the body below" and he thought everything was okay, since he had heard of stories like that before. He stood up and felt pretty good and went to slide open the wooden door when he noticed a milky film over the doorway. He pushed on it and described it as feeling a bit like cellophane. As he walked through it, he knew he was dead.

On the other side of the doorway, everything was in black and white. There was no color or no signs of life anywhere. He desperately tried to find anything in that world that was alive. No grass, no plant, no other people - only death, no signs of life anywhere. Dave had been a Catholic altar boy at one time, and desperately tried to remember one of the prayers he had heard so many times, but nothing came together in his mind. After what seemed like days of struggling, he knew that he couldn't pray and felt even more hopeless than before.

He remembers cars parked with no life and clocks that were stopped as though time just stood still. Nothing moved, not even the wind. It was a horrible place of staleness and death. After no success in finding any signs of life, he sat down by a dark, dingy lake. He picked up a stone and threw it in the dark water and noticed there wasn't even a ripple. No movement, just stale, stagnant death everywhere. David desperately tried to remember a prayer, but realized he had never learned one and couldn't say anything. In his desperation, he called out one word, "Jesus!" and suddenly a man's hand was on his shoulder. It was the first sign of life he had seen since arriving in the morbid abyss. He tried to see who it was, but a power stronger than David kept him from turning around to see. All David remembers was the man's hand on his shoulder. No words were spoken. At that very moment, he was back in the trailer standing in front of the mirror only to realize he had not yet slit his wrist. David threw the knife on the floor and ran into the kitchen to tell his girlfriend and her children that he loved them. She asked him why he was acting so strange. He was afraid no one would believe his story, so he said, "Nothing's wrong."

A couple of weeks after hearing Dave's story, he wrote it out in an email for me, word for word and ended with these words, "Since that night in the trailer, I have never told anyone about this story...until now."

David believes this was a visit to hell, and that Jesus is the One who rescued him from that place of death and mental torment. He believes the spiritual visit to hell spared his life, freed him from the spirit of suicide and that it now can serve as a testimony to set others free. Since this very real supernatural experience, David has turned his life over to Christ. He now resides in Dallas, Texas, where he faithfully attends church with his wife.

No one ever needs to go to hell, if they believe on Jesus as their Lord and Savior.

The Way You Know

> "Let not your heart be troubled; you believe in God, believe also in Me. In My Father's house are many mansions; if it were not so, I would have told you. I go to prepare a place for you. And if I go and prepare a place for you, I will come again and receive you to Myself; that where I am, there you may be also. And <u>where I go you know, and the way you know</u>." Thomas said to Him, "Lord, we do not know where You are going, and how can we know the way?" Jesus said to him, "<u>I am the way, the truth, and the life. No one comes to the Father except through Me</u>."
>
> – John 14:1-6

If you believe Jesus is the Son of God and Savior of the world, you can be saved. It's as simple as ABC — Admit, Believe and Confess.

If you would like to go to heaven, I invite you to pray this prayer today:

> *Dear Jesus, I **ADMIT** that I have sinned. I **BELIEVE** that You died for my sins. Come into my heart and live in me and help me live for You. I **CONFESS** that You are the Lord of my life and I commit my life to serving You.*
>
> *AMEN*

Now find a good church that preaches from the Bible, a church that prays and a church that has a small group that you can join and learn the Scriptures. If we never meet here, I'll see you in heaven!

Notes

1 *"When We All Get to Heaven" by* Eliza E. Hewitt, *pub.*1898. Public Domain

2 "First Day in Heaven" (Stuart Hamblen/Bienstock Publishing Co/Jerry Leiber Music/Mike Stoller Music/ASCAP/Hudson Bay Music Company/BMI/©1953)

3 by John Foxe, *Actes and Monuments*, also known as *Foxe's Book of Martyrs*, published in 1563 by John Day publishing

4 Line made famous by fictional character, Captain James Kirk, in the TV series, "Star Trek".

5 Song title "Heaven's Sounding Sweeter" written by Jimmy Swaggart

6 100,000 talents of gold = 7,500,000 lbs. Gold at today's price = $1,068 per oz. 100,000 talents = $128,160,000,000USD. (gold price @ http://www.monex.com)

1,000,000 talents of silver = 75,000,000 lbs. Silver at today's price = $14.10 per oz. 1 million talents = $16,920,000,000USD. (silver price @ http://www.monex.com)

7 Line made famous by fictional character, Buzz Lightyear, in the movie, "Toy Story".

8 *When We All Get to Heaven*. Eliza E. Hewitt, pub.1898

9 From the Hebrew word 'arown. The Hebrew lexicon is Brown, Driver, Briggs, Gesenius Lexicon; this is keyed to the "Theological Word Book of the Old Testament." These files are considered public domain.

10 *water.usgs.gov/edu/propertyyou.html*

11 *www.myersbriggs.org/*

SOUND ADVICE HAS NEVER BEEN EASIER TO FIND.

Church Trainer is a church consulting ministry that provides training seminars, manuals & leadership development programs for ministers & church leaders.

We offer:
- Strategic planning for church health & church growth
- Inspections & improvements for existing systems in your church
- Staff alignment strategies & solutions
- Training seminars for staff & lay leaders
- Monthly FaceTime coaching sessions
- Coaching cohorts
- Mentoring for new ministers
- Free resources
- & much more!

INFO@CHURCHTRAINER.COM | (888) 366-6498

CHURCHTRAINER.COM

ARMOR BEARERS

STRENGTH AND SUPPORT FOR SPIRITUAL LEADERS

INFO@CHURCHTRAINER.COM | (888) 366-6498
CHURCHTRAINER.COM

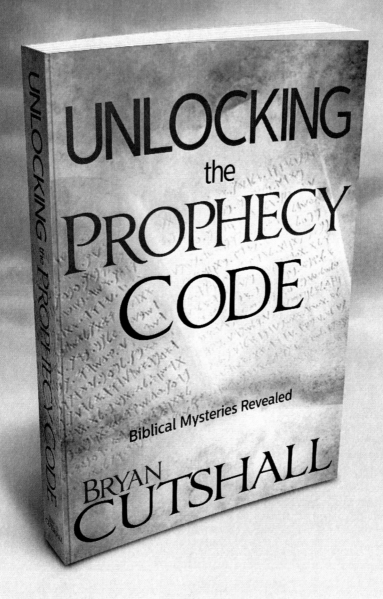